FOR FUNCTIONAL WRITING SKILLS

New English Composition Workbook

Kazuyo Murata

Mami Otani

KINSEIDO

Kinseido Publishing Co., Ltd.

3-21 Kanda Jimbo-cho, Chiyoda-ku,
Tokyo 101-0051, Japan

First published 2021 by Kinseido Publishing Co., Ltd.

Cover design   sein
Text design   Yasuharu Yuki

音声ファイル無料ダウンロード

http://www.kinsei-do.co.jp/download/4128

この教科書で 🎧 DL 00 の表示がある箇所の音声は、上記 URL または QR コードにて
無料でダウンロードできます。自習用音声としてご活用ください。

▶ PC からのダウンロードをお勧めします。スマートフォンなどでダウンロードされる場合は、
　 ダウンロード前に「解凍アプリ」をインストールしてください。

▶ URL は、検索ボックスではなくアドレスバー (URL 表示欄) に入力してください。

▶ お使いのネットワーク環境によっては、ダウンロードできない場合があります。

◉ CD 00　左記の表示がある箇所の音声は、教室用 CD (Class Audio CD) に収録されています。

はしがき

　本書は，*English Composition Workbook* の改訂版です。おかげさまで好評をいただき4回目の改訂をすることができました。旧版にはたくさんの方々から感想をお寄せいただいたことに感謝いたします。改訂にあたっては，「英語が書けるようになるには何が必要か」ということを一番に考えました。「英語を書く」という目標を達成するためには，①単語が書ける，②単語同士をつなぐためのルール（文法）を身につける，③基本的な文を覚えそれを応用する力をつけることが必要です。これらを育成するために，①各ユニットで設定した場面に必要な単語を提示する（Vocabulary for Writing），②各ユニットの目標となる Task に必要な文法をわかりやすく提示する（Grammar for Writing），③各ユニットで必要な基本文を提示する（Key Sentences for Writing）といった工夫をしています。今回の改訂では，目で見て，耳で聞いて，口で読んで，手で書いて，頭で覚える，といった「身体を使って学ぶこと」を意識しています。Key Sentences for Writing，Warm-Up，Grammar for Writing には音声をつけ，英文を耳で聞いて確認し定着させることができるようにしています。また，☑ がついている箇所では単語や例文，解答文をぜひ音読してください。そして音読したら ☑ にチェックを入れましょう。

　New English Composition Workbook は身近にありそうな場面を題材にした 20 ユニットから成っています。各ユニットは次のような構成です。

Key Sentences for Writing　ターゲットとなる基本文です。暗記・暗唱しましょう。

Warm-Up　ターゲットとなる文法事項やタスクに必要な表現を盛り込んだ，皆さんの到達目標となる文章（会話）です。各ユニットの最後には皆さんもこの Warm-Up に出てくるような英語表現を書ける（話せる）ようになりましょう。

Grammar for Writing　ターゲットとなる文法事項の説明です。このテキストで扱う文法事項は必須のものばかりです。必ず習得しましょう。

VOCABULARY FOR WRITING　各ユニットで提示された場面に関連する表現を集めています。

EXERCISE　ターゲットとなる文法事項に関連した練習問題，およびタスクに必要な練習問題です。

TASK 各ユニットで学習したことを駆使して，実際に自分で英文を書いてみましょう。巻末のタスクシートを使ってください。さらに，このタスクで学んだことを利用して，実際に手紙や e-mail を出してみてくださいね。

Tips for Writing いくつかのユニットにあるこのコラムは，各ユニットで提示された場面に関連した tips です。

　私たちは毎年学生にアンケートを実施していますが，学生の皆さんが求める英語の授業とは「実際に役に立つ授業」「楽しく学べる授業」の2つに集約されるようです。このテキストはこの2つを目指して作成しました。そのため，海外旅行や e-mail，あるいは就職活動ですぐに実践できるような場面を設定しました。また，必須の基本的な文法を盛り込むことで，「英文法はややこしくて嫌い」という方にも楽しく学べるように工夫しました。毎回授業の最後には，巻末のタスクシートを使ってタスクをやりとげることで，達成感を感じてもらうとともに，それを切り取って提出することで，教員とのコミュニケーションも図ることができるようにと考えています。

　国際化が加速的に進み，英語はより身近な言語になってきました。さらにインターネットやスマートフォンの普及に伴って，受信はもとより英語での情報発信も必要不可欠になりつつあります。学生たちにとって一番身近なSNS をはじめ，e-mail やビジネス文書，会社でのプレゼンテーションなど，英語を使う機会はますます増えています。このテキストが，皆さんの英語学習のお役に立てば幸いです。そして，ここで学習したことを利用して，ぜひ実際に英語で情報発信をしてくださいね。

　最後になりましたが，本改訂に際しお世話になった金星堂の長島吉成氏に心より感謝いたします。

2020 年 秋

村田　和代
大谷　麻美

CONTENTS

FOR FUNCTIONAL WRITING SKILLS

New English Composition Workbook

UNIT 1 Self-Introduction 自己紹介をする

be 動詞・一般動詞

I'm a college student. I study (　　　　　).

（　　）には自分の専攻を入れましょう。

Warm-Up 3

ニュージーランドにホームステイすることになった Miyabi さんに，ホストファミリーの
Holmes 家の Tessa さんから e-mail が届きました。

Dear Miyabi,

I'm Tessa, the daughter of Tommy Holmes.
Let me introduce myself. I'm a college student.
I go to Te Aro University and study art.
I live with my father, Tommy, my mother, Jane, my sister, Lily.
We have a dog, too. His name is Mickey.
We're looking forward to seeing you, Miya.

Best wishes,
Tessa

◆1分間黙読しましょう。どんな内容でしょうか。

◆英語を書くときに大切なのは主語と動詞です。今日のターゲットは動詞です。動詞に下線
　を引きましょう。

Grammar for Writing 4

📖 be 動詞

英語の動詞には be 動詞と一般動詞があります。be 動詞は，主語によって，is, am, are と
変わります。be 動詞は，イコールの関係を作るので，「**be 同士**」と覚えるとわかりやす
いですね。疑問文と否定文の作り方も覚えていますか。疑問文では be 動詞を前に，否定
文では be 動詞の後ろに not を入れましたね。

- I **am** a student. （I「私」= a student「学生」）
- Tommy **is** an accountant. （Tommy「トミー」= an accountant「会計士」）
- You **are** right. （you「あなた」= right「正しい」）
- **Are** you a student?
- I am **not** a student.

📄 一般動詞

一般動詞は，動作を表します。主語が三人称単数（私とあなた以外の人［もの］で単数）のとき，-s（-es）を付けるのでしたね。疑問文と否定文を作るときには do（does）が必要です。

- I **go** to school.—My sister **teaches** English.
- **Do** you **go** to school?—**Does** Kenji **like** math?
- I **do not (don't) go** to school.—Linda **does not (doesn't) play** tennis.

☑ VOCABULARY FOR WRITING

◆自己紹介に役立つ表現

《学年》

freshman（1 年生） sophomore（2 年生） junior（3 年生） senior（4 年生）

《学部》

Science（理学部） Literature（文学部） Engineering（工学部）
Law/Jurisprudence（法学部） Medicine（医学部）
Commercial Science（商学部） Pharmacy（薬学部） Agriculture（農学部）
Business Administration（経営学部） Economics（経済学部）
Sociology（社会学部） Education（教育学部）
Foreign Study（外国語学部） International Relations（国際関係学部）

《専攻》

linguistics（言語学） literature（文学） social welfare（社会福祉）
psychology（心理学） international relations（国際関係）
policy science（政策学） business (administration)（経営学）
accounting（会計学） biology（生物学） chemistry（化学）
mathematics（数学） environmental science（環境学）

cf. I am a <u>freshman</u> in <u>the Department of Law</u> at ABC University.
I <u>study</u> / <u>major in</u> linguistics.

Tips for Writing

英語で e-mail を書くときの呼びかけと結びのあいさつについて簡単に紹介します。メールの最初に呼びかけを忘れないようにしましょう。親しい間柄であれば John, のように何もつけずにファーストネームで始める場合もありますが，そうでない場合は，Dear Mr. Smith, Dear Ms. Lopez, といったように Dear をつけるようにしましょう。また，メールの最後には結びのあいさつを忘れないようにしましょう。一般的には，Sincerely, Sincerely yours, Regards, Best regards, が使われます。親しい間柄では，All the best, Best wishes, Cheers, Your friend, が使われるようです。「これからもやりとりしようね」ということを伝えたいときには Keep in touch, がよく使われます。

EXERCISE

☑ **1** （　　）の中の適切な語を選びなさい。

1. Hana (has / is) very pretty.

2. My friends (is / are) kind.

3. My parents (live / lives) in Osaka.

4. (Does / Is) your daughter study math?

5. Frank (doesn't / isn't) major in law.

☑ **2** 次の英文の否定文と疑問文を作りなさい。

例）Sayaka is a student. ⇨ *Sayaka is not (isn't) a student. / Is Sayaka a student?*

1. Mai is a teacher.

2. Roy majors in business.

3. Suzan and Mary study art.

4. Eiji speaks German.

5. Mr. Kim lives in San Francisco.

6. Aiko and Kokomi come from Okinawa.

☑ **3** （　　）内の語句を使って，次の日本語の意味を表す英文を書きなさい。

1. 私は経済学を専攻しています。(economics, major in)

2. 私はボストン大学の 3 年生です。(Boston University, junior)

3. 私の両親は山口出身です。(parents, from)

4. 兄は大学院で言語学を学んでいます。(at a graduate school, linguistics)

5. 私は現代美術に興味があります。(modern art, interested in)

☑4 イラストを見て，簡単な紹介文を書きなさい。

例）*Toshiko studies English. She lives in Osaka.*

1. _____

2. _____

3. _____

☑5 ニュージーランドへの入国書類を作成しなさい。機内で渡された入国書類に記入してみましょう。次の情報を使ってください。

◆ ホテル：Four Seasons Hotel Wellington　◆ 出発地：大阪　◆ 飛行便：NZ973
◆ パスポート番号：ML1234567　◆ 滞在期間：7 日間

New Zealand Passenger Arrival Card

1 flight number/ name of ship

passport number

nationality as shown on passport

family name

given or first names

date of birth　day　month　year

occupation or job

full contact or residential address in New Zealand

country of birth

ovrerseas port where you boarded THIS aircraft/ship

2a Answer this section if you live in New Zealand. Otherwise go to '2b'.

• How long have you been away from New Zealand?
years　months　days

• Which country did you spend most time in while overseas?

• What was the MAIN reason for your trip?
○ business　○ education
○ other

• Which country will you mostly live in for the next 12 months?
○ New Zealand　○ other

2b Answer this section if you DO NOT live in New Zealand.

• How long do you intend to stay in New Zealand?
years　months　days
○ permanently or

• If you are not staying permanently what is your MAIN reason for coming to New Zealand?
○ visiting friends or relatives　○ business　○ holiday/ vacation
○ conference/ convertion　○ education　○ other

• Where did you last live for 12 months or more?
country

state, province, or prefecture　zip or postal code

※最新版はニュージーランド税関庁のサイト（https://www.customs.govt.nz/）を参照

📖 TASK

もうすぐあなたの大学に来る交換留学生の Suzan にメールを書きなさい。Key Sentences for Writing を参考に，メールで自己紹介しましょう（→ 85 ページ）。
ヒント：Dear Suzan, で始めて，自己紹介文を書き，I'm looking forward to seeing you soon. で文を終える。

My Family, My Friends

家族や友人を
紹介する

名詞の単数・複数，冠詞，形容詞

Key Sentences for Writing 5

- My father is a very cheerful guy.
- I have two younger sisters.

 6

Susan の家族を紹介した次の文を読んで，下の絵の空欄にそれぞれの名前を記入しなさい。

This is my family. I have two father**s** and **a** mother. When I was young, my father Dick and my mother Rose divorced. After that my mother remarried. My father Dick is **a** very intelligent and elegant man. Though we do not live together, I can see him every weekend. My step-father Robert is **a** nice and cheerful guy. He is always smiling. He loves **beer**. I have two younger sister**s** Sue and Ann. Sue is shy and Ann is very outgoing. They do not resemble each other at all. **The** picture below is **the** most popular one in my family.

 7

📋 名詞の単数・複数，冠詞（a, an, the）

物の名前を表す名詞には，**数えられるもの**（可算名詞—sister, mother など）と**数えられないもの**（不可算名詞—beer, paper など）とがあります。数えられる名詞には，単数を表す **a（an）**や，複数を表す **-s** などが付きます（**a** mother, two sisters）。数えられない名詞には a や -s は付きません（× a beer，× beers）。また可算，不可算名詞ともに次のような場合は前に **the** が付きます。

- 一度言及された名詞（Fukuoka is a big city. The population of **the** city is four million.）
- 特定化された名詞（**the** picture below）
- 最上級（**the** most popular one）
- 序数（**the** first day of **the** 21st century）
- only などで修飾された名詞（**the** only Asian student in this class）

📑 形容詞

名詞を修飾する単語を形容詞と言います。a, the, my, this などの後ろ，名詞の前にくっつきますね。語順を間違えないようにしましょう。

例） a **beautiful** day　that **tall Japanese** girl

2つ以上の形容詞を使用する場合は，おおよそ次のような順序があります。

> 冠詞・所有格－数－性状・新旧・老若－出身・材料－名詞

例） the **two young** boys　my **red cotton** jacket　those **tall American** men

---

☑ VOCABULARY FOR WRITING

◆数と量を表す表現

many と a few は数えられる名詞を修飾します。
　I have **many** friends in **many** countries.
　We have **a few** days before we leave Japan.

much と a little は数えられない名詞を修飾します。
　As Tom drank too **much** beer, he could not walk.
　There is **a little** milk in the refrigerator.

few，little は「ほとんどない」という否定的な意味になります（**a** few, **a** little とは意味が異なります）。
　Very **few** people live to be 100 years old.
　There is **little** hope of his recovering.

some, a lot of は数えられる名詞にも，数えられない名詞にも使用できます。
　some books　**some** tea　**a lot of** people　**a lot of** water

数えられない名詞にも，次のような表現を使用することで数を表すことが可能です。
　a piece of paper　**two slices of** pizza　**a glass of** milk　**two cups of** coffee

---

☑1 ( ) 内に a, an, the のうち適切なものを記入しなさい。また，何も必要なければ ×を入れなさい。

Mr. and Mrs. Smith have ( ) son and ( ) daughter. They live in ( ) wonderful house in ( ) Mississippi. John, ( ) son, is working at ( ) bank, and Mary, ( ) daughter, goes to ( ) college and is studying ( ) commerce. They really live ( ) happy life. But ( ) only concern Mr. Smith has is ( ) Mary's boyfriend. Mr. Smith doesn't like ( ) him because he has ( ) beard and ( ) long hair.

☑2 ( ) の中から適切な語句を選びなさい。

1. My father often gave me (an advice / many advices / much advice) when I was in trouble.

2. NGOs are working to protect (peace / a peace / the peace) in various (areas / area / the area) in the world.

3. As we live in a countryside, we don't need so (much / many / a few) money here.

4. There were so (many / much / few) people in the building that we could not walk.

5. Bob bought (a / a pair of / a piece of) pants at the shopping mall.

6. I could get (many / much / two or three) information about the book in the library.

☑3 ( ) 内の語句を正しい語順に並べ替えなさい。

1. We found a nice restaurant in (new / the / building).

2. In that picture I saw (young / a / woman / American).

3. Whose are (very / shirts / these / dirty)?

4. (her / pretty / three / daughters) look like their father.

5. It is difficult for (older / many / people) to catch up with the information technology.

4 下の形容詞を用いて各人物の特徴を描写する文を作りなさい。書き出しは示してあります。

1. The lady _____

2. That man _____

   • bald   • middle-aged   • thin   • well-built   • plump   • cute   • quiet
   • smart   • curly (hair)   • straight (hair)   • blond (hair)   • friendly
   • talkative   • shy   • sexy   • good-looking

5 音声を聞いて（　　　）を埋めなさい。そしてイラストに各人物の名前を記入しなさい。 8

Let me introduce (　　　　). My best friend is Paul. He is (　　　　) guy.
Joe is (　　　　). He is (　　　　) and is always reading a book. Tom and
Mike are twins. Tom (　　　　　) than Mike. Mike likes to (　　　　)
so that everyone can identify him. Alex comes from Mexico. I like (　　　　).

🗊 TASK

家族や友人の写真を用意し，Warm-Up を参考にして写っている人の特徴を英語で説明しなさい（85 ページ）。

> **Key Sentences for Writing**
> - There is a desk by the window.
> - There are two DVDs on the table.

イラストを見て，下の文の（　）に適当な語を入れなさい。（　）内は 1 語とは限りません。

This is a picture of my room.

There is a desk (　　　　) the window.

There is a bed (　　　　) the desk.

There is a computer (　　　　) the desk.

There is a cat (　　　　) the desk.

There is a dresser (　　　　) the desk and there are a lot of cosmetics (　　　　) the dresser.

There are a T-shirt and a skirt (　　　　) the floor.

How untidy my room is!

Grammar for Writing

there 構文

Unit 1 では be 動詞はイコールの関係を表すことを確認しました。しかし，be 動詞は「…がいる，…がある」という「存在」の意味を表すこともあります。「…がある」は **There is a 単数名詞**（＋場所），**There are 複数名詞**（＋場所）という構文で表します。

- **There is** a book on the shelf.
- **There are** a lot of students from abroad in my class.

ひとつのもの（人）の存在を表す場合は is (was)，複数の場合は are (were) を使います。
この there 構文は目に見えて「そこにある」もの（人）を表すばかりではありません。

- **There is** a tip on how to save money.
- **There must be** a solution to the problem.
- **There is** nothing to worry about.
- **There are** over 6,000 languages in the world.
- **There was** a good movie last night.
- **There's** something wrong with it.
- **There can be** no doubt about it.

疑問文では be 動詞を主語の前に出し，否定文では「be 動詞＋not」にします。

- **Is there** anything that you cannot eat or drink?
- **There isn't** a department store in this town.

ただし，名詞に定冠詞（the）や所有格（my, your, her, Larry's など）が付く場合，there
構文を使わないことに注意しましょう。

- **The book is** on the desk.（× There is the book on the desk.）
- **My room is** on the second floor.（× There is my room on the second floor.）

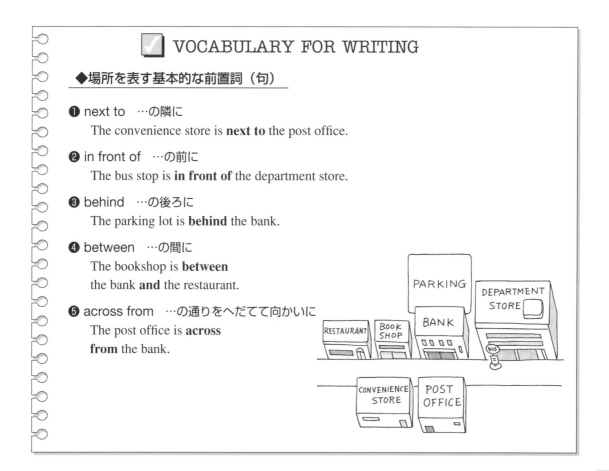

✅ VOCABULARY FOR WRITING

◆場所を表す基本的な前置詞（句）

❶ next to　…の隣に
The convenience store is **next to** the post office.

❷ in front of　…の前に
The bus stop is **in front of** the department store.

❸ behind　…の後ろに
The parking lot is **behind** the bank.

❹ between　…の間に
The bookshop is **between**
the bank **and** the restaurant.

❺ across from　…の通りをへだてて向かいに
The post office is **across**
from the bank.

☑ 1 下の図はホテルの１階の平面図です。この図を見て下の文の（　）に適当な語句を記入しなさい。

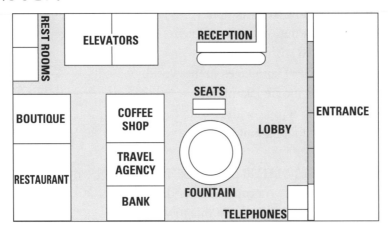

1. There is a (　　　　) next to the (　　　　).
2. There are some (　　　　) in front of the (　　　　).
3. There is a (　　　　) between the (　　　　) and the (　　　　).
4. There are (　　　　) in the corner of the (　　　　).
5. The (　　　　) is behind the (　　　　).
6. The (　　　　) is in the center of the lobby.

☑ 2 下の表を見て，この学校の過去・現在・未来の姿を "there was (were)" "there is (are)" "there will be" の文を使って２つ書きなさい。

	1970	now	2040
students	2,300	3,000	3,200
teachers	160	190	170
campuses	2	3	3

e.g. There were 2,300 students in 1970. There are 3,000 students now.
There will be 3,200 students in 2040.

1. _____

2. _____

☑3 Box 1 と 2 から 1 語ずつ選んで，1 から 5 の日本語の意味を表す英文を作りなさい。

BOX 1

a little water, few restaurants,
little money, little water, much
money, my car, the famous church

BOX 2

in my town, in the bank,
in the garage, in the refrigerator,
on the top of the hill

1. その有名な教会は丘の上にあります。

2. 冷蔵庫に少し水があります。

3. 私の町にはレストランがほとんどありません。

4. 銀行には大金があります。

5. 私の車はガレージにあります。

4 音声を聞いて，もっとも適当な絵を a, b, c の中から選び，記号で答えなさい。なお，音声はそれぞれ 2 回ずつ読まれます。 **12**

1. _____ a)  b)  c)

2. _____ a)  b)  c)

もう一度音声を聞いて，（　　）を埋めなさい。

1. There is (　　　　　　　　　　　　　) the window.

2. There is (　　　　　　) across (　　　　　　　　　　).

◎TASK

87 ページのタスクシートに Key Sentences for Writing を応用して，自分の理想の部屋を 5 つ以上の文章で描写しなさい。また，ペアを組んで自分の文章を読み合い，相手の「理想の部屋」のイラストを書きなさい。

Everyday Activities

スケジュールを
説明する

現在形・現在進行形

> **Key Sentences for Writing** 13
>
> - I always wake up at 7 a.m.
> - I sometimes work part-time at a restaurant after school.

 14

Weekday's Routine

6:00 A.M.	wake up
7:00 A.M.	get dressed
7:30 A.M.	leave for school
9:00 A.M.	arrive at school
10:00 A.M.	be in school
12:30 P.M.	eat lunch
4:00 P.M.	leave school
5:30–7:30 P.M.	work part-time at a tennis school on Monday and Friday
8:30 P.M.	come home
9:00 P.M.	have dinner
10:00 P.M.	watch TV / relax
11:00 P.M.	take a bath
12:00 A.M.	do homework
1:20 A.M.	go to sleep

上の表を見て，（　　）に適する語句を入れなさい。（　　）内は1語とは限りません。

I (　　　　　　　　) at 6:00 a.m.

I (　　　　　　　　) school at 7:30 a.m.

After school I work at a tennis school (　　　　　　　　).

I (　　　　　　　　) before I (　　　　　　　　).

I (　　　　　　　　) after midnight.

 15

現在形と現在進行形

現在形は現在の状態を表したり，反復的・習慣的な行動を表す場合に使います。

- What time **do** you usually **get up**?
- I usually **get up** at 7:00 a.m.
- My mother **plays** tennis every Sunday.

× I'm watching TV every night.

（「毎晩見る」というのは習慣的な動作を表すので進行形では不適切）

現在進行形は，be 動詞 + -ing 形の動詞という形で，「（今）…している」という意味です。疑問文では be 動詞を主語の前に出し，否定文では「be 動詞 + not」にします。

- Our daughter **is studying** English in her room.
- **Is** our teacher **having** lunch at a cafeteria?
- My father **isn't taking** a bath now.

know, consist などの状態を表す動詞は現在進行形にできないことに注意しましょう。これらの動詞は辞書では「状態動詞」と表記されていたり，「進行形は不可」といった注意が記されています。

× I'm not knowing her name.

 ## VOCABULARY FOR WRITING

◆頻度を表す表現

頻度を表す副詞（句）（副詞については Unit 6, 22 ページ参照）

always		100%	いつも
almost (nearly) always		95%	ほとんどいつも
usually, regularly		80–90%	通常，たいてい
often, frequently		75%	よく
sometimes		50%	ときどき
occasionally, once in a while		25–40%	時折，たまに
seldom, rarely		10%	めったに（…しない）
never		0%	全然（…しない）

頻度を表す副詞 always, sometimes などは通常，一般動詞の前，be 動詞の後ろに位置します。

I **always** go to bed at 11.
Children are **often** afraid of the dark.

その他の頻度を表す語句

every day（毎日）　every week（毎週）　every weekend（週末ごとに）
once a week（週に 1 回）　once a month（月に 1 回）　once a year（年に 1 回）
twice a week（週に 2 回）　three times a month（月に 3 回）
four times a year（年に 4 回）　many times a year（年に何度も）

頻度を尋ねるには how often を使います。
　　cf. **How often** do you play tennis?—I play tennis once a week.

EXERCISE

☑ **1** ２つの文の意味を比べ，その違いを説明しなさい。

1. (a) I always check social media at night.
    (b) I am checking social media now.

2. (a) I do not eat breakfast on weekends.
    (b) I am not eating breakfast now.

3. (a) Do you watch TV every day?
    (b) Are you watching TV now?

☑ **2** 次の質問に（　　）内の語句を使って答えなさい。ただし動詞は適切な形に変えなさい。

1. What do you usually do after dinner? (play games)

2. What are you doing now? (do homework)

3. How often do you get your hair cut? (once a month)

4. What time do you usually wake up? (at 6:30)

5. Are you cooking spaghetti? (No, Japanese noodle)

☑ **3** 次の文の間違いを訂正しなさい。

1. I am knowing his name.

2. We are understanding the story.

3. Can you wait? I take a shower now.

☑ **4** あなた自身の日常について，14 ページの Warm-Up に出てくる表現や下のヒントを参考にしながら文を完成させなさい。

I always (   ) at home.
I usually (   ) in my free time.
I often (   ) after school.
I sometimes (   ) over the Golden Week.
I seldom (   ).
I never (   ).

> **ヒント**
> drink coffee, drive a car, go back home, listen to music,
> smoke, take a bath, take a trip, watch videos/TV

☑5 ( ) 内の語句を使って，次の日本語の意味を表す英文を書きなさい。

1. サトシはいつもビールを飲むが，今はワインを飲んでいる。(beer, wine)

2. あなたはふだんどんな音楽を聞いていますか。(what kind of music)

3. タカコはめったに中華料理を作らない。(Chinese food, cook)

4. ルーシーは健康のために毎朝ジョギングをしている。(to stay fit, every morning, jog)

5. 私は週に3日，コンビニでアルバイトをしている。(at a convenience store, work part-time)

6 音声を聞いて，女性が美しさを保つためにしていることを下から選び，該当するイラストに○を記入しなさい。 🔊 **16**

a.

b.

c.

d.

e.

f.

g.

h.

i.

次の英文は，答えの根拠となった文です。もう一度音声を聞いて，( ) を埋めなさい。

1. I ( ) to stay fit. **2.** I ( ) sweet.
3. I ( ) as possible. **4.** I ( ) early.

📖 TASK

87ページの表に一日のスケジュールを記入しなさい。また，それについて説明する文を，Key Sentences for Writing を参考に5つ作りなさい。

Recipes

レシピを書く

他動詞・自動詞

Key Sentences for Writing 17

- Cut the tofu in cubes.
- Boil the soup stock and add soy sauce.

 18

何のレシピでしょうか。

Number of people: *1 serving*
Preparation time: *15 minutes*

Ingredients:

80 g	*Chicken*
1/3 cup	*Dashi or soup stock*
1 1/2 T.	*Japanese soy sauce*
1 T.	*Mirin, or sake*
1/2 T.	*Sugar*
1/4	*Onion*
1	*Egg*

Cut the chicken into cubes. Cut the onion into thin rings. Boil the soup stock and add the soy sauce, *mirin* or *sake*, and sugar. Boil it again. Add the chicken and simmer for five minutes. Add the onion and simmer for one minute. Stir the eggs in a bowl. Add the eggs into the pan and simmer for two minutes. Put it on hot rice in a bowl.

 19

他動詞と自動詞

「…を」（目的語）が必要な動詞を他動詞，そうでない動詞を自動詞と言います。

□内の語句が目的語です。自動詞の文では目的語がないことに注目しましょう。

他動詞

- Sandy cuts | the pork roast |.　　| 豚肉を |切る
- Bob boiled | the vegetables |.　　| 野菜を |ゆでる

自動詞

- The stock boils.　　　　　出し汁が | × |沸騰する。
- The potatoes are frying.　ジャガイモが | × |揚がっている。
  - *cf.* I fried | the chicken |.　　私は| 鶏肉を |揚げた。
    （この場合は fry を他動詞として使っていますね）

自動詞には前置詞句が伴うことがよくあります。これらの語句は目的語ではないので，前置詞を忘れないようにしましょう。

- My father listens <u>to classical music</u>. （× My father listens classical music.）
- We arrived <u>at the hotel</u>. 　　　　　（× We arrived the hotel.）
- My teacher talked <u>about the issue</u>. 　（× My teacher talked the issue.）

また他動詞の中には日本語の意味からは自動詞と紛らわしいものがあるので気をつけましょう。

- They discussed the merits of opening a new airport .
  （× They discussed about the merits . . .）
- Tommy married Kathy .
  （× Tommy married with Kathy.）
- My daughter wants to become a teacher .
  （× My daughter wants to become to a teacher.）

辞書では，他動詞は他， T ， t.v. （transitive verb），自動詞は，自， I ， i.v. （intransitive verb）という表記があります。fry のように，他動詞・自動詞の両方の使われ方をする動詞もあります。

Tips for Writing

命令文は，いつも「…しなさい」と訳していませんか。必ずしも命令ではなく「行為を指示する文」として働きます。命令以外に，レシピや道案内（→ Unit 20 参照），取扱説明書などに用いられます。
- Press the button to start the machine. （自動洗車機のインストラクション）
- Do not wash any items in an automatic dishwasher. （ミキサーの取り扱い説明書）

☑ VOCABULARY FOR WRITING

◆料理に関係ある表現

a bottle of orange juice　1 本のオレンジジュース

a can of soup　ひと缶のスープ

a six-pack of coke　6 本 1 パックのコーラ

a carton of eggs　卵 1 パック

a bag of flour　小麦粉ひと袋

a loaf of bread　パン 1 斤

a pinch of salt　塩ひとつまみ

a teaspoon (tsp) of sugar　砂糖小さじ 1 杯　5 cc

a tablespoon (tb) of salt　塩大さじ 1 杯　15 cc

a cup of milk　牛乳 1 カップ　約 240 cc （*cf.* 日本では 1 カップ＝200 cc）

EXERCISE

✓**1** 次の文の間違いを訂正しなさい。

1. We discussed about the issue.

2. Will you marry with me?

3. Let's enjoy at the party.

4. Did you attend to the meeting yesterday?

5. The divorce rate raised last year.

6. I'm waiting you.

7. Tom entered into the room.

8. Alice replied him.

✓**2** 次の表現を英語にしなさい。

1. 砂糖小さじ1杯
2. 小麦粉カップ1杯
3. 食パン1斤
4. ピザひと切れ
5. 卵1パック
6. 塩ひとつまみ
7. 大さじ1杯のオイル
8. コーラ1本
9. 6本入りビール
10. クッキー1箱

✓**3** 料理に関する動詞を選びなさい。

1. カレーを作る	(	) curry	**a.** bake
2. サラダを作る	(	) salad	**b.** cook
3. 魚を焼く	(	) fish	**c.** eat
4. 卵焼きを作る	(	) eggs	**d.** fry
5. 目玉焼きを作る	(	) sunny-side up	**e.** grill
6. 野菜炒めを作る	(	) some vegetables	**f.** make
7. パンを焼く	(	) bread	**g.** measure
			h. weigh

8. ケーキを焼く　　　　　　　(　　　　　　) cake

9. 材料を量る
   （カップやさじを使う場合）（　　　　　　) the ingredients
   （はかりで計量する場合）　（　　　　　　) the ingredients

4 次の日本語を英語の指示文になるよう語句を並び替えて文章を完成させなさい。

1. お米は炊く1時間ぐらい前に洗って水気を切っておきます。(cooking / the rice / dry off / the water / rinse / before / and / about an hour)

2. なべに水を入れて火にかけます。(a pan / and / heat / into / some / water / put / it)

3. 豆腐を4センチ角に切ります。(cubes / the tofu / four-centimeter / into / cut)

4. ニンジンの皮をむき千切りにします。(cut / into / and / thin / it / strips / long / a carrot / peel)

5. 野菜をドレッシングであえます。(the vegetables / the dressing / mix / with)

5 音声を聞いて（　　）に□の中の語から適当な語を入れてレシピを完成 🔊 **20** させなさい。完成させたら，何のレシピか日本語で書きなさい。

1. (　　　　　　) tuna, boiled eggs, cucumber, tomatoes and olives in a
   (　　　　　　) bowl. (　　　　　　) the dressing on them and toss them well.
   (　　　　　　) for 30 minutes in the refrigerator, then garnish with chopped
   (　　　　　　).

2. (　　　　　) the (　　　　　) into small pieces. (　　　　　) a little salt and
   pepper. (　　　　　) some (　　　　　). (　　　　　) the flour, water, eggs and
   cabbage together. (　　　　　) a frying pan with some oil in it. (　　　　　)
   the pork and pour the mixture onto the pork. (　　　　　) it on both sides
   until lightly browned.

> parsley　add　mix　chill　pork　shred　cut
> heat　cabbage　fry　bake　pour　salad　mix

🔲 **T A S K**

Key Sentences for Writing を参考に，豆腐の味噌汁の作り方を英語で書きましょう。89ページのレシピに記入しなさい。

Introducing My Town 私の街を紹介する

副詞・比較級・最上級

Key Sentences for Writing 21

- Nara is a smaller town than Kyoto.
- Kyoto is the most popular tourist site in Japan.

✎ Warm-Up 22

比較級に下線を，最上級に波線を引きなさい。

I live in the Kansai region in Japan. In this area there are several very interesting cities to visit. Kyoto is the most popular tourist site in this area. There are so many old temples and shrines there. On the other hand, Osaka is the busiest city in Kansai. You can visit so many fashionable shops and good restaurants there. Nara is much smaller than those two cities, but it is the oldest capital in Japan. Please try to visit Nara Park. It's very beautiful. If you are planning to visit Kansai, spring and fall are the best seasons. You can enjoy beautiful flowers in spring and autumn leaves in fall.

✎ Grammar for Writing 23

📋 副詞

副詞とは動詞，形容詞，副詞，文全体などいろいろなものを修飾する語です。

- I want to carry it **around**. （動詞 carry を修飾）
- This sells **well**. （動詞 sell を修飾）
- Mary is a **very** smart girl. （形容詞 smart を修飾）
- His answer is **completely** wrong. （形容詞 wrong を修飾）
- Marc can speak English **fairly** well. （副詞 well を修飾）
- **Unfortunately** the team lost the game. （文全体 the team lost the game を修飾）

📋 比較級・最上級

形容詞と副詞は，2 つのものを比べて「より…」という意味の**比較級**に，3 つ以上のものを比べて「最も…」という意味の**最上級**にすることができます。

比較級には形容詞，副詞の後ろに **-er** を付けます。**than** を付けて「…よりも」と比較する対象を表すこともできます。

- Do you have a small**er** one **than** this?
- The time passes fast**er** as I get older.

-ly で終わる語（例外 early）や 3 音節以上の語には -er の代わりに **more** を用います。
- Could you speak **more** loudly?
- Sunday will be **more** convenient than Saturday for me.

最上級には形容詞，副詞の後ろに **-est** を付けます。比較対象を表すために「…の中で・うちで」の意味で **among** を付けることもあります。
- Lake Ontario is the small**est** lake **among** the Great Lakes.
- He works hard**est** in his company.

-ly で終わる語や 3 音節以上の語には -est の代わりに **most** を用います。
- Who can speak Spanish **most** fluently in this class?
- This is the **most** important problem among these.

✅ VOCABULARY FOR WRITING

以下はちょっとややこしい比較級，最上級です。きちんと整理して覚えておきましょう。

		比較級	最上級
good	（形容詞　良い）		
well	（形容詞　元気な 副詞　うまく）	**better**	**best**

例）● Chicken is **better** than beef for our health.（良い）
　　● He can sing **better** than any other students.（うまく）

		比較級	最上級
bad	（形容詞　悪い）		
ill	（形容詞　病気の）	**worse**	**worst**
badly	（副詞　下手に，ひどく）		

例）● This is the **worst** accident in my life.（悪い）
　　● The boy injured **worst** among the classmates.（ひどく）

many	（形容詞　たくさんの）		
much	（形容詞　たくさんの 副詞　とても）	**more**	**most**

例）● I need to read **more** books to write this report.（たくさんの）
　　● Tom spends **more** money for his cell phone than people usually do.（たくさんの）

☑ **1** 文中から副詞を選びなさい。

1. He died happily.

2. He went to school very early in the morning.

3. Buses often come late at this bus stop.

4. The boy was reading books alone in the dark room.

5. Sometimes Japan is hit by a heavy typhoon in summer and fall.

☑ **2** 適切な語句を選びなさい。

1. Canada is (more large / larger / largest) than the United States.

2. In Japan there are (many / much / more) people than in Korea.

3. English is (not difficult / less difficult / difficult) than Chinese for me.

4. The (most / best / more) popular rock group among these is the Rolling Stones.

5. The temperature in Kyoto is higher (than Tokyo / than in Tokyo / among Tokyo).

6. The Everest is (highest mountain / the highest mountain / the higher mountain) in the world.

☑ **3** 指示に従って英文を書き換えなさい。

1. Speaking English is easy for me. （than writing English を付けて比較級に）

2. This is interesting. （of the three videos を付けて最上級に）

3. I feel good today. （than yesterday を付けて比較級に）

4. Nothing is more delicious than caviar in this world. （最上級を使って同じ意味に）

5. New York is the busiest city in the world. （No other city で始めて同じ意味の文に）

4 音声を聞いて，（　　　）に聞き取った表現を書き入れなさい。　🔊 24

1. Tokyo is (　　　　　　　　　　　　) in Japan.
2. Tokyo Disneyland has (　　　　　　　　　　　) Tokyo DisneySea.
3. (　　　　　　　　　　), Tokyo Tower or Yokohama Landmark Tower?
4. Tokyo is (　　　　　　　　　　) in Kanto region, but it has
   (　　　　　　　　　　) in Japan.
5. Roppongi is (　　　　　　　　　　　　) in Tokyo.

5 下記の情報を見て，比較級や最上級を用いてこれらの村を比較する文を3つ作りなさい。

	South-Bay Village	Richmond Village	Inglewood Village
Population	3,120	1,200	6,500
Area	210 km^2	450 km^2	55 km^2
Temperature in August	18℃	32℃	28℃
Temperature in January	3℃	-5℃	22℃
The number of crime/year	1	3	12

_____

_____

_____

TASK

Warm-Up を参考に，近隣の町と比較しながら，あなたの住む町を 89 ページに紹介しなさい。

Asking Questions

質問をする

wh 疑問文

Key Sentences for Writing 25

- What do you do after classes?
- How many hours do you sleep?

 Warm-Up 26

下記は「若者の生活様式」についてのアンケートです。答えてみましょう。

This is a survey about your lifestyle.

① How many classes do you have a week?
    a) less than 5   b) 5-9   c) 10-14   d) more than 15

② Where do you study mainly?
    a) at home   b) at a library   c) in a computer room   d) at a lab
    e) others

③ What do you do after classes?
    a) sleep   b) study   c) work part-time   d) have a date
    e) club activity   f) others

④ How many hours do you sleep?
    a) less than 4   b) 4-5   c) 6-7   d) 8-9   e) more than10

⑤ Who do you live with?
    a) by myself   b) with my family   c) with my boy/girlfriend
    d) with my roommate

 Grammar for Writing 27

wh 疑問文

yes/no の答えではなく，具体的な情報を答えとして求める質問をするときには **what,
who, which, when, where, why, how** などの疑問詞を使います。疑問詞のあとの語順は，
主語の前に助動詞や動詞がきます。

- **Where** is the beauty salon?—It is in Harajuku on Meiji Street.
- **Who** is that man in black?—He is the Vice-President of the United States.
- **What** should I do in case of an emergency?
    —You should stay calm and find an exit.
- **Which restaurant** do you recommend in this town?
    —I recommend Jack's Steak House.
- **When** does the school year begin in Japan?—It begins in April.
- Tom, **how** was this week?—It was terrible. I had the flu and stayed in bed.

疑問詞が主語となる疑問文

疑問詞が主語になる場合（誰が，何が，どちらがなど）は，その後ろは平叙文と同じ語順になります。
- **Who** broke the vase?—My mother broke it.
- **Which** class is the most popular among students?
    —Dr. Simpson's class is the most popular among them.
- **What** is wrong?—This telephone number is wrong.

✓ VOCABULARY FOR WRITING

◆ how で始まる疑問文

疑問詞 how のあとには，次のような形容詞や副詞が付くことがあります。

《how + 形容詞》
   How tall are you?
   How much is it?
   How much money do we need to buy the premier ticket?
   How many people were killed by the terrorism?
   How long is the Nile?
   How old is the Diet Building of Japan?
   How far is it from your house to your university?

《how + 副詞》
   How often do you have snow in Tokyo?
   How long does it take from Tokyo to Kyoto by Shinkansen?
   How much do you love me?
   How soon does she come home?

EXERCISE

☑1 下の文が答となるように，(　　　) に適切な語句を入れて疑問文を作りなさい。

1. Q: (　　　　　　) does it take from L.A. to Tokyo?

A: About nine hours.

2. Q: (　　　　　　) is the population of Japan?

A: About 120 million.

3. Q: (　　　　　　) do you come to the library?

A: Two or three days a week.

4. Q: (　　　　　　) is the main cause of global warming?

A: The pollution.

5. Q: (　　　　　　) was the weather in Hong Kong?

A: It was fine.

6. Q: (　　　　　　) of these plans do you like best?

A: I like this one.

☑2 次の単語を並べ替えて正しい文を作りなさい。

1. (your / school / in / English / teaches / who)?

2. (who / with / you / the park / to / go / did)?

3. (so / what / you / happy / made)?

4. (the United States / days / many / you / did / in / how / stay)?

5. (how / like / the video / you / did)?

☑3 下のイラストを参考に疑問文を作りなさい。

1.   **2.**   **3.**   **4.**

1. _____

2. _____

3. _____

4. _____

4 これはトムの1週間の予定です。この表を参考にして，彼の行動について下の日本文
に沿ってもっと詳しく尋ねてみましょう。

Tom's calendar	
Sunday	Date with Jane
Monday	Go to a library　　　Part-time job
Tuesday	University classes
Wednesday	University classes
Thursday	University classes　　Pick up his younger sister at a nursery
Friday	Part-time job　　　Pay day!
Saturday	Watch videos

1. ジェーンとどこに行くの？

2. 図書館で何をするの？

3. いくつ授業をとっているの？

4. 何時に妹のお迎えに行くの？

5. お給料っていくらくらいもらえるの？

6. ビデオは何本くらい見るの？

5 音声の質問を聞いて，自分自身のことを英語で答えなさい。　🔊 28

1. I'm (　　　　　　) years old.

2. _____

3. _____

4. _____

5. _____

⧉ TASK

Warm-Up を参考に，ゴールデンウィークをどう過ごしたかについてのアンケート質問を91 ペ
ージに作成しなさい。そして，それをクラスメートと交換して回答してもらいましょう。

5 文型・過去形

> **Key Sentences for Writing** 29
>
> • I read a book yesterday.
> • I found the book interesting.

Warm-Up 🔊 30

それぞれの文の動詞に下線を引きなさい。

Today was a wonderful day. I woke up and got up at 5:00. It was really fine outside and I took a walk to the park. There were a lot of flowers and they were very beautiful. When I came back, the morning walk made me so hungry that the breakfast tasted more delicious than usual. As I had much time before leaving, I made lunch for me and for my father. I took the earlier train and arrived at school 30 minutes before the first class began. I prepared for the class, so I really enjoyed it. I found the following proverb true: "The early bird catches the worm."

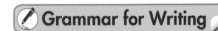 Grammar for Writing 🔊 31

📑 基本 5 文型

第 1 文型 S（主語）＋ V（動詞）「…（S）は…する」
目的語がないので動詞は自動詞ですね。

- I walked.
  S　V
- The elevator stopped.

第 2 文型 S（主語）＋ V（動詞）＋ C（補語）「…（S）は…だ」
主語＝補語の関係になっています。この文型の代表的な動詞は be 動詞です。

- Today is my birthday.
  　S　 V 　　C
- The flowers were beautiful.

第 2 文型を作るのは，be 動詞以外では，become, seem, look, sound, taste などがあります。動詞の後ろに目的語があるように思えるかもしれませんが，主語＝補語の関係になるので，目的語ではありません。

- He looked happy. (he = happy)
  S　 V 　　C
- She became a lawyer. (she = a lawyer)

第3文型　S（主語）+ V（動詞）+ O（目的語）「…（S）は…（O）を…する」

目的語をとる他動詞の文ですね。第2文型と異なるのは動詞を挟んだ2つの語句（主語，目的語）が，イコールの関係にならない点です。

- I read a newspaper. (I ≠ a newspaper)
  S   V   O
- I canceled my appointment. (I ≠ my appointment)

第4文型　S（主語）+ V（動詞）+ O（目的語）+ O（目的語）

「…（S）は…（O）に…（O）を…する」／「…（S）は…（O）を…（O）に…する」

「…を」という目的語（直接目的語）以外にもうひとつ「…に」という目的語（間接目的語）をとります。

- I sent you an e-mail. (= I sent an e-mail to you.)
  S   V   O   O
- My boyfriend ordered me a new dress.
  (= My boyfriend ordered a new dress for me.)
- He asked me a favor. (= He asked a favor of me.)

第5文型　S（主語）+ V（動詞）+ O（目的語）+ C（補語）

「…（S）は…（O）を…（C）に…する」

目的語（O）= 補語（C）の関係になっています。

- I called Tomoyuki Tommy. (Tomoyuki = Tommy)
  S   V   O   C
- The song made me happy. (me = happy)
- I found the book difficult. (the book = difficult)

第4文型と似ていますが，第4文型では2つの目的語がイコールの関係ではありませんね。

- He offered Mike a job. (Mike ≠ a job) …第4文型

📄 過去形

過去形は，過去の動作や状態を表します。

be 動詞

be 動詞の過去形は was と were の2つです。

- They **were** junior high school students five years ago.
- The concert **was** great.

一般動詞

通常，動詞の語尾に -ed や -d を付けます。疑問文，否定文には did が必要です。

- I **enjoyed** the movie.
- I **liked** him.
- **Did** you **go** to school yesterday?
- No, I **didn't go** there and stayed at home all day.

不規則な変化をする動詞（e.g. go—went, bring—brought）もチェックしましょう。

EXERCISE

✓ 1 正しい方を選びなさい。

1. **A.** Mike breaked the window.   **B.** Mike broke the window.
2. **A.** They didn't lose their keys.   **B.** They didn't lost their keys.
3. **A.** What did everybody do?   **B.** What was everybody do?
4. **A.** Who was he talked to?   **B.** Who did he talk to?
5. **A.** I did not play football.   **B.** I was not play football.

✓ 2 同じ文型を選び記号で答えなさい。

1. Mary will appear soon.   (   )   **a.** Keith is a teacher.
2. The flower smells good.   (   )   **b.** I'll get you a ticket.
3. Suzan washed her car.   (   )   **c.** What made you so angry?
4. Kazu bought her a present.   (   )   **d.** He came yesterday.
5. They named their baby Sally.   (   )   **e.** We take three meals a day.

✓ 3 ヒントを参考に次の質問に英語で答えなさい（動詞を過去形にするのを忘れないようにしましょう）。

What did you do yesterday? Write three things you did yesterday.

1. _____
2. _____
3. _____

> **ヒント**
> check my e-mail, drink coffee/tea, drive a car, eat breakfast/lunch/dinner,
> go to school, have a date, play tennis, watch TV, work part-time

✓ 4 次の指示に従って英文を書き換えなさい。

1. Does she like the food?（過去形に）

2. I went shopping today.（否定文に）

3. Tom called up <u>his sister</u> on his cell phone.（下線部を尋ねる疑問文に）

4. I gave him the book.（第 3 文型の文に）

5. I feel sad because of the news.（made を使った第 5 文型の文に）

5 音声を聞いてイラストをストーリーの順番に並べ替えなさい。 32

a.  b.  c.  d.

e.  f.  g.  h.

(　　) → (　　) → (　　) → (　　) → (　　) → (　　) → (　　) → (　　)

6 もう一度音声を聞いて（　　）に適当な動詞を書きなさい。 33

On Thursday afternoon I (　　　　) to the Hankai Department Store to
(　　　　) some shopping and to (　　　　) a friend for dinner. In the Cosmetics
Department I (　　　　) a lipstick. Then I (　　　　) the elevator to the third
floor. In the Ladies' Fashion Department I (　　　　) a handbag and a belt.
When I was waiting for the elevator, I (　　　　) a silk scarf. I (　　　) it
on and (　　　　) that it (　　　　) me nicely. I (　　　) to (　　　) it
and (　　　　) around for a salesclerk. I (　　　　) the time and (　　　)
that I (　　　　) late for my appointment. I (　　　　) a checkout counter and
(　　　　) to it and (　　　　). The elevator (　　　　) and I (　　　) it
to the sixth floor. I (　　　) out of the elevator and (　　　　) to the Hana
Grill. When I (　　　　) there, my friend (　　　　) me and (　　　　). We
(　　　) a wonderful dinner and (　　　) a good time.

Key Sentences for Writing を参考に，日記を書いてみましょう（91 ページ）。

UNIT 9 Making a Reservation

予約のメールを書く

未来形 / would like to

 35

メールの用件は何ですか。また未来を表す表現，希望を表す表現に下線を引きなさい。

From:	"Shoichi TAKEMOTO"<take@pwc.net.jp>
Date:	
To:	"Uli Candolo" <glacier@grindel.ch>
Subject:	Room availability and rates for August 9 to 12

Dear Sir or Madam,

We are going to stay at Grindelwald this summer. Our friends stayed at your hotel and recommended it to us. We would like to know about room availability and room rates. Please send us some information about your hotel for the period indicated below.

From Aug. 9 to12 (three nights)

We are a family of three, a couple and a 5-year-old daughter. We would like to stay in a room with a bath and with a view of the Eiger.

Shoichi TAKEMOTO
take@pwc.net.jp

Grammar for Writing 36

📄 will, be going to

未来を表す場合は，will + 動詞の原形あるいは，be going to + 動詞の原形を使います。be going to は，前から考えていることや計画していること，あるいは明らかにそうなるであろう，という場合に使います。

- It **will** probably be cold tomorrow.
- Look. It is dark outside. It's **going to** rain.
- I have a sore throat. I'm **going to** catch a cold.
- Sharon **is going to** have a baby next month.

疑問文・否定文は次のようになります。

疑問文 ● **Will** it **be** cold tomorrow? (Yes, it **will**. / No, it **won't**.)
　　　 ● **Is** it **going to** rain? (Yes, it **is**. / No, it**'s not** [it **isn't**].)
否定文 ● It **won't** (= will not) be easy.
　　　 ● She **is not going to** quit her job.

📋 未来を表す現在進行形

tomorrow, next week のように，もっと近いうちに行われることについて述べるときには，現在進行形（be 動詞 + -ing 形の動詞）を使います。この場合には，その計画や予定の準備が進んでいることや，約束や取り決めがされているということを表します。

　● Jesse **is leaving** Australia for Japan tomorrow night.
　● A famous soccer team **is arriving** from Italy.
　● **Are** you **coming** to the party tonight?

📋 would like to

「…したいのですが」といった希望を丁寧に伝えるときには would like to + 動詞の原形という表現を使います。

　● I **would like to** stay for two nights.
　● We **would like to** take a cab to the airport.
　● I**'d** (= I would) **like to** talk to Mr. Harrison, please.

Tips for Writing

will は未来を表す以外に「…しよう」という意志を表すことに注意しましょう。
　● I gained a lot of weight. I will go on a diet.
　● I won't follow her.
　● I will go there whatever happens.

☑ VOCABULARY FOR WRITING

◆ホテルの予約に役立つ表現

シングルルーム（シャワー付き・バスタブ付き）a single room (with a shower / with a bathtub)
ツインルーム（シャワー付き・バスタブ付き）a twin room (with a shower / with a bathtub)
ダブルルーム（シャワー付き・バスタブ付き）a double room (with a shower / with a bathtub)
スイートルーム（寝室・浴室のほかに居間などがある）a suite room
山側の（山の景色の見える）/ 海側の（海の見える）/ 街側の
　　　　　　　　　　　　　with a mountain view / with an ocean view / with a city view
禁煙室　a nonsmoking room

EXERCISE

☑ 1 be going to か will を使って文を完成させなさい。

1. Suzan (   ) have a baby next month.

2. I hope you (   ) like my present.

3. Look at those clouds. It (   ) rain.

4. I (   ) see the doctor tomorrow at 10:00.

5. Perhaps we (   ) meet again someday.

6. I think I (   ) take piano lessons in the near future.

☑ 2 今週の Tom のスケジュールを見て，例を参考に be going to を使った文を３つ以上作りなさい。

例）Tom is going to have dinner with Kathy this Sunday.

Sunday	dinner with Kathy
Monday	June's birthday party at night
Tuesday	tennis school
Wednesday	a business meeting at 5:00 p.m.
Thursday	fitness club after work
Friday	*Star Wars* (ABC cinema) with Mike
Saturday	visit my parents

1. _____

2. _____

3. _____

☑ 3 ヒントを参考に「…しよう」「…しないようにしよう」という意志を表す文を will と won't を使って３つずつ書きなさい。

例）I will study English every day. I won't sit up late.

> **ヒント**
> learn another language, drink, smoke, do regular exercise,
> clean my room every day, study harder, work part-time,
> belong to a sports club

<will> 1. _____

         2. _____

         3. _____

<won't> 1. _____

2. _____

3. _____

4 夏休みに海外旅行をすることになりました。❶誰とどの国へ行きますか。❷どの都市でどれくらい滞在しますか。❸何がしたいですか。例文の（　）を自由に変えて書きなさい。

例文） This summer I am going to (Switzerland) with (my family). We are going to stay in (Grindelward) for (five days). We would like to (go hiking there) and (enjoy the mountain views).

_____

_____

_____

_____

_____

_____

_____

_____

5 ホテルの予約に役に立つ表現です。日本語にあうように，語句を並び替えて文を完成させない。

1. ホテルのことはインターネットで見つけました。(found / your hotel / the Internet / we / on)

2. 私たちは3人で全員女性です。(all / we / of / female / and / three / a party / are)

3. 私たちは，バス付きのトリプルルームで禁煙室を希望します。(room / a triple / to / with / would like / a bathtub / we / stay / nonsmoking / at)

📖 **TASK**

Key Sentences for Writing を使って，ホテルの予約をするメールを書いてみましょう（93ページ）。

Writing a Postcard

旅先からはがきを
書く

受動態

┌─ **Key Sentences for Writing** ─┐

• I'm excited to see such a wonderful castle.

• It was built 100 years ago.

 **Warm-Up**

下のはがきの文中にある受動態に下線を引きなさい。

Oct. 12, 2011   AIRMAIL

Dear Satoshi:

I am in Nara now. I went to Todaiji
temple yesterday. It was built in
the Nara period. I was amazed to
see the big Buddha. It is made of
metal. I saw a lot of deer near the
temple.
I also visited the National
Museum. A lot of old treasures were
displayed. It was very crowded.
Your country is beautiful. I wish
you were here!

Best wishes,

Kathy

Satoshi SATO

P.O. Box 385
Olally WA 38799
U.S.A.

 **Grammar for Writing**

📋 **受動態**

受動態（受け身）は「…が…される」を表す文です。be 動詞＋過去分詞が基本の形です。
「誰によって」という行為の主体は，通常 by... で表します。

● Our meals **are prepared by** my mother. (= My mother prepares our meals.)

● This picture **was taken by** Takako. (= Takako took this picture.)

行為の主体が不明な場合，あるいは重要でない場合は，by 以下が省略される場合も多く
あります。

● These clothes **are made** in China.

● The temple **was built** more than 1,000 years ago.

助動詞を含む文では助動詞＋be 動詞＋過去分詞，進行形の場合は be 動詞＋being ＋過
去分詞となります。

● The new coffee shop **will be opened** next week.

● My watch **is being repaired**.

受動態で表す感情表現

感情を表す表現に受動態が使われることがあります。日本語の感覚とは異なることが多いので注意が必要です。

- be delighted at（…に喜ぶ）
  They **were delighted at** the good news.
- be satisfied with（…に満足する）
  We **are satisfied with** the restaurant's service.
- be surprised at（…に驚く） I **was surprised at** the news.
- be annoyed at/with（…に怒る） She **was annoyed at** the interruption.
- be embarrassed by/at/about（…に困惑する）
  The mother **was embarrassed by** her son's bad behavior.
- be bored with（…にうんざりする／飽き飽きする）
  I'**m bored with** her complaints.
- be tired of（…にうんざりする／飽き飽きする）
  I'**m tired of** doing house chores.
  cf. be tired from（…に疲れる） I'**m tired from** walking too much.

Tips for Writing

日付の書き方は，アメリカとイギリスとでは異なります。

	アメリカ式	イギリス式
年 月 日	December 15, 2020	19th May, 1965
	12/15/20 or 12.15.20 （年数の最初２ケタは省く）	19/5/(19)65 or 19.5.(19)65
読み方	December fifteenth, twenty twenty	the nineteenth of May, nineteen sixty-five

✓ VOCABULARY FOR WRITING

◆絵はがきに使える便利な表現

It's highly **recommended**.	（お薦めだ）
It **was packed**.	（超満員だった）
It **was** really **crowded**.	（とても込んでいた）
It **was** almost **empty**.	（がらがらだった）
It **was filled with** tourists.	（観光客でいっぱいだった）
We **were** very **tired**. / We **were worn out**.	（へとへとだった）
You should have been there.	（来ればよかったのに）
I wish you were there.	（あなたがいたらよかったのに）
I wish you had come.	（あなたも来ていればよかったのに）

1 ( ) の中の適切な語を選びなさい。

Disneyland (open / opened / was opened) by Walt Disney in 1955 at Anaheim, California. It (divides / is divided / is dividing) into several different "lands" such as Adventure Land, Frontier Land and Tomorrow Land, and also (have / has / is having) hotels, restaurants and shops. Tokyo Disneyland (built / was built / was building) in 1983. It (is included / includes / included) similar attractions to the original Disneyland. DisneySea (was opened / was open / was opening) in 2001 and (is located / located / is locate) next to Tokyo Disneyland. Both parks (are visited / visit / visited) by people from all over the world.

2 次の文の間違いを訂正しなさい。

1. Basketball was invent by Naismith.

2. I was surprising at the news.

3. Gorillas found in Central Africa.

4. The package will send to Susan tomorrow morning.

5. A big shopping mall is being building now.

6. The store is crowding with shoppers all the time.

3 ( ) に適当な語を入れて文を完成させなさい。それぞれの文には ⬚ の中の動詞を適当な形に変えて使います。

1. I ( ) ( ) in 1965.
2. Spanish ( ) ( ) in most of Central and South America.
3. The theater will ( ) ( ) next spring.
4. Lady Gaga's new song will ( ) ( ) next week.
5. Baseball ( ) ( ) between two teams of nine players.
6. Stamps ( ) ( ) in most convenience stores.
7. We ( ) ( ) with the TV programs last night.
8. Her leadership is ( ) ( ) now.

a.	question
b.	bore
c.	close
d.	bear
e.	play
f.	release
g.	sell
h.	speak

4 次の語句を使って受動態の文を作りなさい（ただし，動詞を適当な形に変え，適当な前置詞を加える必要があります）。

1. the news / surprise / be / I

2. the traffic jam / annoy / be / we

3. the good result / delight / will be / she

4. excite / the discovery of a new planet / be / they

5. tire / eating the same fast food / be / he

5 下のイラスト1から3について，A，B，Cの3つの文が読まれます。そのうち各イラストの内容と合っているものをひとつ選んで記号で答えなさい。 40

❶ ❷ ❸

もう一度音声を聞いて，（　）を埋めなさい。

1. A. The hotel was built (　　　　　).
   B. The hotel was built (　　　　　).
   C. The (　　　) being repaired.
2. A. The address of (　　) is 1856 South Street.
   B. (　　　　　　).
   C. (　　　　　) was established in the (　　　　).
3. A. (　　　　　　) the drawings.
   B. (　　　　　　) the exhibition.
   C. (　　　　　　) the museum.

◻ TASK

Key Sentences for Writing を参考に，旅先から絵はがき（93ページ）を書いてみましょう（受動態の文を少なくとも1文は入れてください）。

助動詞 can / be able to

Key Sentences for Writing | 41

- I can drive a car.
- I can use a computer.

 42

Keiko さんの履歴書です。

Keiko Sakamoto

3-2-5 MM Apartment #516
Ryoma Street, Fushimi-ku,
Kyoto, 608-3852
(075) 666-888

Objective
■ Position as Accounting Clerk

Education
■ 2011–2014 ABC University, Kyoto

Skills
■ Computer Skills: Word, Excel,
  Power Point, Access
■ Language Skills: English, Japanese,
  a little Chinese

Qualifications
■ Book keeping 2nd grade
■ Driver's license

References
■ Available upon request

Keiko さんのできることは何ですか？（　　）を埋めてみましょう

- She (　　) use a computer.　• She (　　) keep accounts.
- She (　　) speak (　　　　　) and a little (　　　　).
- She can (　　　　) a car.

 Grammar for Writing | 43

📑 助動詞 can

can は「…ができる」という能力や可能性を表します。can の後ろには動詞の原形が来ます。否定形は cannot (can't)，疑問文は Can S（主語）＋動詞 ...? ですね。過去形には could / could not (couldn't) を使います。

- Kathy **can** speak German very well.
- Roy **cannot** speak German at all.
- **Can** he speak French? Yes, he **can**. / No, he **can't**.
- Mitsuhiro **could** walk when he was a year old.

📋 be able to

be able to も can と同じように「能力」を表します。疑問文では be 動詞を主語の前に出し，否定文では「be 動詞 + not」にします。

- Helen **is able to** communicate with people well.
- I **was not able to** find the book anywhere in my house.
- **Are** you **able to** provide the technical assistance we might need?
- He **is not able to** visit Japan during that period.

can はほかの助動詞と一緒に使ったり，不定詞と一緒に使ったり，完了の have と一緒に使ったりすることはできません。このような場合には，can の代わりに be able to を用います。

- Mark <u>will</u> **be able to** join our party. (× will can join . . .)
- I want <u>to</u> **be able to** speak Chinese. (× want to can. . .)
- I <u>have</u> never **been able to** sing karaoke well. (× have never can . . .)

📋 can を使った慣用表現

can の疑問文には次のような用法があります。

許可を請う表現
Can I . . . ? や Could I . . . ? は「…してもいいですか」と自分が何かをしてもいいか尋ねる文としても使えます。Could I . . . ? の方がより丁寧です。

- **Can I** ask you a personal question?
- **Can I** join the tennis club?
- **Could I** borrow your dictionary?

依頼の表現
Can you . . . ? や Could you . . . ? は「…してもらえますか」という依頼文としても使えます。Could you . . . ? の方がより丁寧です。

- **Can you** clean up our room?
- **Can you** turn on the TV?
- **Could you** tell me the way to the station?

Tips for Writing

履歴書はアメリカ英語では Resume，イギリス英語では CV です。 Resume / CV は，日本の履歴書と違って，特に決まった書式はないようです。一般的には，Personal Data（氏名，住所，電話番号，メールアドレス等），Objective（希望職種），Education（学歴），Skills（技能，特技），Work Experience（職歴），Qualifications（資格），References（照会先：日本の保証人にはあたらず，本人の資質を保障できる，大学のゼミの先生や以前の職場の上司）が書かれます。

EXERCISE

✓1 （　　）の中の適切な語を選びなさい。

1. We (will can / will be can / will be able to) travel to space in the future.

2. (Can / Are / Do) you help me with this fax machine?

3. I hope (can / to can / to be able to) play the guitar.

4. Sally has never (could / been able to / could have) understand her boss.

5. Frank (can / was can / could) walk when he was 10 months old.

✓2 （　　）の指示に従って文を書き換えなさい。

1. Katsu can play the piano. （by the time he was 6 を付けて過去の文に）

2. Kathy can speak Japanese. （soon を付けて未来の文に）

3. I can choose my own career. （want to を加えて「…できるようになりたい」という文に）

4. Can you type more than 100 words per minute? （be able to の文に）

5. I cannot phone my parents. （have と yet を使って「ずっと…できないでいる」という文に）

✓3 （　　）内の語句を使って，次の日本語の意味を表す英文を書きなさい。

1. 彼女は1週間ほどで歩けるようになるでしょう。（in a week or so）

2. もう少し大きな声で話してもらえませんか。（could, speak loudly）

3. どうすればこの窓を開けられますか。（how, this window, open）

4. 切符は観光情報センターで買うことができます。（tickets, from the Tourist Information Center）

5. コンピューターが使えなければなりません。（you, use a computer）

4 次の仕事をするために必要なことについて述べなさい（ヒント以外の表現を使っても構いません）。

ヒント
be beautiful
be friendly
dance
memorize a lot of streets
ski
use a cash register

例）Delivery person
⇨ You must be able to ride a motorcycle.

1. Kindergarten teacher:
⇨ You must be able to

2. Sports instructor:
⇨ You must be able to

3. Shop clerk:
⇨ You must be able to

4. Model:
⇨ You must be able to

5. Taxi driver:
⇨ You must be able to

5 音声を聞いて，（　）を埋めなさい。それぞれが何を説明しているか答えなさい。 44

1. It's very convenient especially when you (　　　　).
(　　　　　　), a shop, or a hotel (　　　　　　　).
You don't need to (　　　　　) when you carry it with you.

2. You (　　　　) a variety of things here. Cosmetics and women's accessories (　　　　　　). There are many types of restaurants (　　　　).

3. (　　　　　　), fruits, meats, and fish fresh in it.
(　　　　　　) because ice cream is sometimes in it.

◎TASK

Key Sentences for Writing を参考に，アルバイトに応募するため，95 ページのデータシートを記入しましょう。can や be able to を使って自分の持っているスキルをアピールしましょう。

Writing a Letter

フォーマルな手紙を
書く

to 不定詞

Key Sentences for Writing 45

- I hope to see you next week.
- I go to London to study English.
- Please let me know some good books to read.

 **Warm-Up** 46

次の手紙を読んで，文中の to 不定詞に下線を引きなさい。

> 4-6 Nishi-cho, Sagamihara,
> Kanagawa 228-0825 Japan
>
> May 22, 2011
>
> British Museum
> Great Russell Street, London
> WC1 B 3DG U.K.
>
> Dear Sir or Madam,
>   I am interested in your museum, and am planning to attend your
> short programs to study Egyptian history. I would be very grateful if
> you could send me a catalog of your programs. I would be grateful if
> you could let me know some books to read before the program, too.
> I am looking forward to hearing from you.
>
>   Sincerely yours,
>   Ryutaro Kagawa

 **Grammar for Writing** 47

📑 to 不定詞

to 不定詞とは動詞（原形）の前に前置詞 to が付いたもので，名詞，形容詞，副詞とよく
似た働きをします。to 不定詞の 3 つの基本的な用法を確認しておきましょう。

(1) 名詞的用法 =「…すること」
名詞のように文の主語や補語，目的語として働きます。
- | **To** study a foreign language | is not easy for me. （主語）
- The aim of this trip is | **to** see a lot of historic places in China |. （補語）
- I hope | **to** see you | next week. （目的語）

(2) 副詞的用法＝「…するために」「…して」「…するには」

動詞や形容詞を修飾する副詞のような働きをします。

■ 目的「…するために」
- I went to Osaka to see him .（to see him が went を修飾）
- I am writing to thank you for your gift.（to thank you が am writing を修飾）

■ 原因「…して」
- I was happy to hear the news .（to hear the news が happy を修飾）
- His teacher was disappointed to read his report .（to read his report が disappointed を修飾）

■ 意味範囲の限定「…するには」
- The system was very difficult to understand .（to understand が difficult を修飾）
- He is easy for me to work with .（to work with が easy を修飾）

(3) 形容詞的用法＝「…すべき」「…する」

名詞を修飾する形容詞のような働きをします。
- I have a lot of things to do .（to do が things を修飾）
- I have a lot of good friends to help me .（to help me が friends を修飾）
- Do you have something to write with ?（to write with が something を修飾）

Tips for Writing

英語でフォーマルな手紙を書く際は，次のような形式を取ります。

差出人の住所
日付

受取人の名前
受取人の住所

Dear ..., 注1

本文

結語 注2
自筆署名

注1　My dear Tom, Dear Smith Family などの表現もあります。 受取人の名前が明らかでないときは，Dear Sir or Madam を使うと便利です。

注2　結語には，Sincerely yours, With regards, With best wishes, With love などを使用します。

EXERCISE

✓1 Warm-Up の文中の to 不定詞はそれぞれ，Grammar for Writing で説明した３つのどの用法でしょう。

1. _____
2. _____
3. _____

✓2 （　　）の中に入る適切な表現を下から選びなさい。

1. The best way to find a girlfriend/boyfriend is (　　　　　　　　).
2. My sister entered the university (　　　　　　　　).
3. I don't have enough room in my house (　　　　　　　　).
4. Try not to eat just before you go to bed if you want (　　　　　　　　).
5. I read three papers (　　　　　　　　).

> **a.** to attend a party　**b.** to study economics　**c.** to lose weight
> **d.** to put another new computer in　**e.** not to be behind times

✓3 ヒントを使って，次の日本語の意味を表す英文を書きなさい。

1. 私は卒業後，留学したいと思っている。

   I want _____.
   > ヒント：「卒業後」= after graduation　「留学する」= study abroad

2. その大学に入るには TOEFL を受ける必要がある。

   You need to _____.
   > ヒント：「入る」= enter　「TOEFL を受ける」= take the TOEFL test

3. ロンドンは音楽の勉強をするにはとてもいいところです。

   London is _____.

4. （あなたから）お便りをいただいてとてもうれしいです。

   I am very _____.
   > ヒント：「…から便りがある」= hear from…

5. このマニュアルはとてもわかりやすい。

   This manual is _____.

✓ 4 to 不定詞を使ってひとつの文にしなさい。

1. The Prime Minister of Japan visited Korea. He was going to see the Korean President.

2. I was very disappointed. I learned that he could not pass the entrance exam.

3. Tom has decided. He will study medical science in the United States.

4. I will study law in the United Kingdom. I want to be a lawyer.

5 会話を聞いて，正しい内容を表すものを選びなさい。　 48

1. Yoko will go to NY _____.
    a) to get a cheap airline ticket
    b) to be a journalist
    c) to study English

2. Tom's advice is _____.
    a) to go to an English conversation school
    b) to find an American friend
    c) to improve English

3. He was surprised _____.
    a) to hear her speak good English
    b) to hear her speak about her summer vacation
    c) to hear her say "Thank you"

音声を聞いて正解を確認しましょう。　 49

📖 TASK

Warm-Up を参考にして，英語学校に手紙を書きましょう (95 ページ)。以下の 3 つのことを内容に入れてください。下線部を表すために to 不定詞を使いましょう。

- 将来イギリスの大学に入学するために夏休みの間ロンドンで英語を勉強したいと思っている。
- 夏の間滞在する寮（dormitory）があるかどうかを尋ねる。
- 学校のカタログを送ってほしい。
  あて先 : 171 Regent Street, London W1R 6BQ UK
  　　　　Dorchester English Academy

Key Sentences for Writing 🔊 50

- You have to be careful after dark.
- You should not walk around at midnight.

✏**Warm-Up** 🔊 51

次の文はニューヨークの旅行ガイドブックの記述です。どのようなアドバイスが書かれてありますか。アドバイスの部分に下線を引いてみましょう。

Some Tips on NYC

At JFK airport in New York, you had better take a yellow cab or a limousine bus downtown. You should not take an unlicensed taxi. They will overcharge you.

It is generally safe in Manhattan in the daytime. But you have to be careful after dark. You should not walk around late at night.

At a hotel or a restaurant, you must tip the bellboy or the waiter/waitress. But you do not have to pay much. Just 10 or 15 percent of the total will be enough. At a fast food restaurant, you do not have to tip at all.

Enjoy a safe trip to New York!

✏**Grammar for Writing** 🔊 52

📋 助動詞 should / must / had better

相手にものごとを勧めたり，忠告する表現には，**should**, **must**, **had better** などを使用します。これら助動詞の後ろには動詞の原形が続きます。

had better：「…しなさい」「…した方がいい」という強い忠告や警告を表します。

- You **had** (You'**d**) **better** take an umbrella. It's going to rain.
- I'**d better not** take any more of your time.

must：「…しなければならない」「…すべき」という命令や義務を表します。

- We **must** take a rest for the next few days.
- **Must** I leave here by tomorrow?
- You **must** visit our house sometime.（親しい間柄で用いる強い勧誘）

should：「…すべき」「…した方がいい」といった勧告や忠告をするときに使います。

- You **should** see a doctor about that cough.

- **Should** I leave a tip?
- We **should not (shouldn't)** bring up those topics.

📋 have to

厳密には助動詞ではありませんが，**have to** も助動詞と同じような働きをします。must と同じような「…しなくてはならない」という意味を持ちます。

- You **have to** show your passport.
- Do we **have to** pay now?
- I **had to** wait for an hour.

must と have to は否定文になると，まったく異なる意味になるので注意が必要です。

- You **don't have to** pay now.（…する必要がない）
- You **must not** use these facilities without permission.（…してはならない）

📋 助動詞 might (may) / could (can)

助動詞 **might** や **could** も，ものごとを勧める助動詞として使われます。ただし，should, must, had better に比べて遠回しな，したがって丁寧な「…してはどうか」という表現になります。

- You **might** like to have a walk around the town.
- You **could** come and stay with us.

Tips for Writing

(1) 強制力の強弱

これらの「聞き手にものごとを勧める助動詞」には，相手への強制力に違いがあります。

強い		You had better	[…しなさい]
		You must	[…しなくてはならない]
		You should	[…すべき]
		You have to	[…しなくてはならない]
弱い		You might/could	[…してはどうか]

話し手との関係や話題の重要性から判断してどの表現を使用するかを考える必要があります。You had better... は相手に有無を言わせない強い意味になることが多いので，年上の人や立場が上の人にはあまり使用しない方がいいでしょう。

(2) アドバイスが欲しいときは？

逆にアドバイスを求めるときは What should I do? を使います。

- I cannot finish my report. **What should I do?**—You **should** talk to the professor.

EXERCISE

☑ 1 日本語の意味になるように（　　）に適切な語句を入れなさい。

1. You (　　　　　　　　　) cook tonight. （今夜は料理しなくてもいいですよ）

2. If you have a fever, you (　　　　　　　　　) go out today. （外出しない方がいいですよ）

3. You (　　　　　　　　　) get out of the room without my permission. （室外に出ては
いけません）

4. (　　　　　　　　　) I pay now? （支払った方がいいですか）

5. I (　　　　　　　　　) go now. （そろそろ行かなくては）

☑ 2 （　　）の指示に従って文を書き換えなさい。

1. She must prepare her meal herself. （yesterday を付けて過去の文に）

2. Don't leave the door open. （must を使った文に）

3. Do some exercise if you want to stay fit. （had better を使った文に）

4. You should stay <u>at the Park Hotel</u>. （下線部を問う疑問文に）

5. No, you don't have to stay in this room. You could go out if you want to. （こ
の文が答えとなる疑問文を）

☑ 3 （　　）内の語句を使って次のような忠告をしましょう。

1. 弟にあなたのコンピューターに触ってはいけないことを伝えましょう。 (touch my
computer)

2. 友人に甘いものを食べ過ぎないように忠告しましょう。 (eat, sweets, too many)

3. 彼氏とけんかをしている友人に，メールを送った方がいい，と言ってあげましょう。
(send him an e-mail)

4. 親にうそをついている友人に，本当のことを話すようアドバイスしてみましょう。
(tell your parents the truth)

4 和代はイギリスへ旅行することになり，イギリス人の Cathy に旅のアドバイスを求めています。会話を聞いて，持っていった方がよいものを下の絵から選びなさい。 🔊 **53**

1. _____ a.   b.   c.

2. _____ d.   e.   f.

3. _____ g.   h.   i.

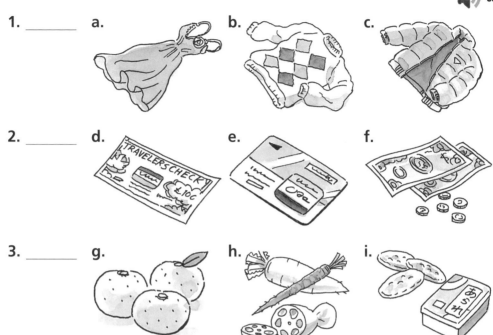

🗐 TASK

夏休みに来日予定の Judy が以下のように e-mail でアドバイスを求めています。3 つの質問それぞれに，Key Sentences for Writing を応用してアドバイスをしてあげましょう (97 ページ)。

Hi. It's Judy. How are you? I plan to visit Japan next summer. Could I ask some questions to help me plan my trip? I would appreciate it if you could give me some advice.

First, I am wondering where I should go. Which town should I go to? What should I see there?

Secondly, I am looking forward to trying some Japanese dishes. What do you recommend? What should I try? Do you know some good restaurants to visit?

Lastly, I hear that it is so hot and humid in summer in Japan. What kind of clothes should I bring with me? Should I bring a long-sleeved shirt or a warm jacket?

I'm looking forward to your reply. Bye-bye!

Judy

Key Sentences for Writing 54

- Would you help me with my report?
- I would like you to give me a ride.

Warm-Up 55

パーティーに大学の教授も招待したいと思います。招待状の文面をもう少し丁寧にするにはどうしたらいいでしょう。表現を変えた方がいいと思われる個所に下線を引きなさい。

We are having a surprise party for Kim to celebrate her 20th birthday. Come and join us for dinner and dancing on the 22nd of October at 7 o'clock.

Location: Roy's Restaurant
Address: 18, 42nd Street, Westwood

Grammar for Writing 56

📋 助動詞 would

would は，助動詞 will の過去形ですが，丁寧で控えめな表現によく使われます。「もしよければ」というニュアンスになります。

依頼の表現

Unit 11 で Can you . . . ? / Could you . . . ? が依頼の表現であることを学習しましたね。Would you . . . ?（Will you . . . ?）も同じように「もしよければ…していただけませんか」という依頼の表現になります。

- **Would (Will) you** help me with my report?
- **Would (Will) you** do me a favor?

Would you . . . ? は Will you . . . ? に比べ，より丁寧な表現になります。また **Would you mind doing . . . ?** はさらに丁寧になります。

- **Would you mind** pick**ing** me up at the airport?

相手の意向・希望を尋ねる表現

Unit 9 で would like to が「…したいのですが」と話し手の希望を述べる表現であることを学習しました。「…してはいかがですか」「…しませんか」と，相手の意向・希望を尋ねるには，**Would you like to + 動詞の原形...?** という表現を使います。

- **Would you like to** go fishing with me?
- **Would you like to** have some coffee?
  * Would you like some coffee? と言うこともできます。

希望・意向を伝える表現

「（人）に…していただきたいのですが」という希望を丁寧に伝えるときは，**would like + 人 + to + 動詞の原形**という表現を使います。

- I **would like** you **to** give me a ride to the station.
- I'**d like** her **to** show me the way to the theater.

Would you like + 人 + to + 動詞の原形...? は「…しましょうか」と相手の希望や意向を尋ねたり何かを勧めたりする表現になります。

- **Would you like** me **to** get you something to drink?
- **Would you like** him **to** call you back?

Tips for Writing

Would you . . . ? (Could you . . . ?) と尋ねられたときは，どのように返答すればいいのでしょうか。

(1) 依頼に対する返答

Would you lend me some money?

yes の場合：Sure. / Certainly. / No problem.

no の場合：I'm afraid I can't. / I wish I could, but I can't.

(2) 何かを勧められた場合

Would you like to have another piece of cake?

yes の場合：Yes, please. / Sure. Thank you.

no の場合：No, thank you. I'm full. / No, I'm fine. Thanks anyway.

☑ 1 （　　）の中に入る適切な語句を下から選びなさい。

1. (　　　　　　　　　　　) a cup of tea?

2. (　　　　　　　　　　　) come to our party next Friday?

3. (　　　　　　　　　　　) have some drink before dinner.

4. (　　　　　　　　　　　) to make a reservation for you?

5. (　　　　　　　　　　　) for breakfast?

6. (　　　　　　　　　　　) come to my office at 3:00 p.m.

a. I'd like to　**b.** I'd like you to　**c.** Would you please **d.** Would you like　**e.** Would you like me　**f.** What would you like

☑ 2 次の各文を would を使って丁寧な表現に書き直しなさい。

1. Show me how to use this vending machine.

2. I want to hear from you more often.

3. I want you to introduce me to that beautiful girl over there.

4. What do you want to eat for dinner tonight?

5. Do you want to come to lunch next weekend?

6. Can you speak a little bit more slowly?

7. I want your help, if you don't mind.

3 次の電話会話の（　　　）を聞き取って記入しなさい。　🔊 **57**

1. Mary: Hello, John. Listen. Our boss wants to talk about our new project.
He wants to see me next Wednesday. But I don't want to go alone.
(　　　　　　　　　　　)?

John: OK. I'll do that.

Mary: Thank you, John. (　　　　　　　　　　　).

2. **Tom:** Hello, Mary. (   ) to a barbecue party next Sunday.
   Mary: Wow, thank you, Tom. That sounds interesting. (   )?
   Tom: That's very kind of you. (   ) for the kids?
   Mary: Sure. No problem. See you on Sunday.

3. **Mary:** Hello, Bob. (   ) a favor for me. I have to buy
             some things for a barbecue party. But unfortunately, my car is not
             running now. (   )?
   Bob: OK. How can I help you?
   Mary: (   ) to the supermarket to buy some soda on
             Saturday afternoon?
   Bob: Sure. No problem.

4 次の e-mail は学生から教授宛てのものです。丁寧な形式に変えなさい。

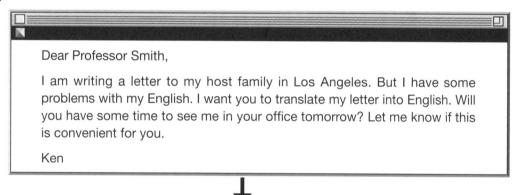

Dear Professor Smith,

I am writing a letter to my host family in Los Angeles. But I have some problems with my English. I want you to translate my letter into English. Will you have some time to see me in your office tomorrow? Let me know if this is convenient for you.

Ken

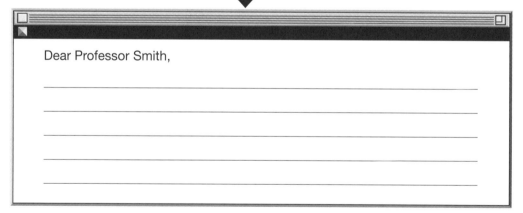

Dear Professor Smith,

_____

_____

_____

_____

_____

📖 TASK

クラスメートの Maki がアメリカ留学のため日本を出発します。お別れ会 (farewell party) に教授も招待しようと思います。Warm-Up を参考にして、パーティーの日時と場所を決めて教授への招待状を書きなさい (97 ページ)。

 58

Key Sentences for Writing

- Don't let your child run in the library.
- Make your child be quiet here.

 59

次の会話のうち，使役文に下線を引きなさい。

Pat: Ken, what's this?

Ken: Can't you read it? You should not let Beverly touch my computer!!

Pat: Did she really touch it? She is only 5 years old.

Ken: She must have touched it. I'm sure she pushed some buttons while I was in the living room watching a comedy show on TV. She made my important file disappear. I cannot believe it!!

Pat: Didn't you copy the file onto a CD-R?

Ken: I think I did, but that one has gone. I wonder where it is.

Pat: I always tell you to keep your room clean. And you shouldn't have left your computer on while you were not here.

Ken: OK, OK. Anyway, don't let her use my computer!!! Make her use her toy computer!!

Notice!
Don't let Beverly
touch it!
Ken

✎ Grammar for Writing 🔊 60

📄 使役文

使役とは，「… (人) に… (動作) をさせる (させてあげる)」という意味を持つ文です。「使役動詞 (make, let, have) + O (目的語) + 動詞の原形」という文型になります。

動作を強制する場合 [make + 目的語 + 動詞の原形]

- The mother **made** her small daughter **wear** a hat. (= The daughter **must** wear a hat.)
- I cannot **make** my husband **stop** smoking.

make はものやこと (無生物) を主語にしてよく使用されます (この場合は「無理やりに」という意味ではなく，原因や理由を表します)。

- What **made** you **decide** to become a doctor?
- This medicine will **make** you **feel** better.

動作を許可する場合 [let + 目的語 + 動詞の原形]

- The mother **let** her child **play** outside. (= The child can play outside.)
- **Let** me **introduce** myself.

make と let の意味の違いは次の文でわかりますね。

- The parents **let** <u>their child</u> **eat** the cake. But they made him brush his teeth after eating it.
- Lucy's parents **let** <u>her</u> **go** to the party. But they made her come home by 10 o'clock.

使役動詞 have [have + 目的語 + 動詞の原形]
目上の者が目下の者に「…させる」という場合や，お金を払うなどしてその職業の人にサービスを提供させる場合に使い，「…させる」と「…してもらう」の両方の意味を持ちます。

- I'll **have** <u>someone</u> **put** these things away.
- I'll **have** <u>a repairman</u> **fix** my computer.

✅ VOCABULARY FOR WRITING

◆コンピューター関係の単語

1. cable　ケーブル
2. disk drive　ディスク ドライブ
3. memory　メモリー
4. screen　スクリーン
5. keyboard　キーボード
6. mouse　マウス
7. program; application プログラム／アプリケーション
8. printer　プリンター
9. laptop　ラップトップ（ノートパソコン）
10. desktop　デスクトップ
11. electric mail; e-mail 電子メール

Tips for Writing

使役文はほかの動詞で言い換えることができます。

My mother **makes** me **clean** my room every day.
= My mother <u>forces</u> me <u>to clean</u> my room every day.
We cannot **let** her **carry out** the plan.
= We cannot <u>allow</u> her <u>to carry</u> out the plan.
I **had** a porter **carry** my luggage.
= I <u>got</u> a porter <u>to carry</u> my luggage.

EXERCISE

☑1 (　) に make, let のいずれかを入れなさい。

1. Advertisers want to (　　　　) you buy things you don't need.

2. Could you (　　　　) me know your schedule by Thursday?

3. Can you ask your boss if she'll (　　　　) you leave earlier?

4. (　　　　) me help you carry your luggage.

5. Sandra doesn't (　　　　) anybody drive her car.

6. Does this pink T-shirt (　　　　) me look fat?

7. We are sorry to (　　　　) you change your plans, but we don't have any tickets tonight.

☑2 (　) 内の語句を並べ替えて文を完成させなさい。

1. The teacher (every week / 50 new words / us / learn / made).

2. Susan's mother (with us / her / come / let / won't).

3. (me / help / let / you) with that bag.

4. I'll (your luggage / the porter / bring / have) up right away.

5. The model (take / her picture / had / a professional photographer).

☑3 次の文を make, let のいずれかを使って同じ意味になるように書き直しなさい。

1. If you take this medicine, you will feel better.

2. Bad weather forced the pilot to cancel the flight.

3. Why did you decide to come to this university?

4. Young children force their parents to use too much time and energy.

5. She won't allow her husband to watch soccer games on TV.

✓ 4 あなた自身のことについて次の文を完成させなさい（ヒント以外の表現を使っても構いません）。

1. When I was an elementary school pupil, my mother did not let me . . .

2. When I was a junior high school student, my parents made me . . .

3. My boyfriend/girlfriend doesn't let me . . .

ヒント
clean my room, drink coffee, go shopping alone,
sit up late at night, smoke, study hard, work part-time

5 音声を聞いて 1 から 3 までの会話はどこで話されているか，a から f の中 から選びなさい。

1. _____ **a)** **b)** **c)**

2. _____

3. _____ **d)** **e)**  **f)**

もう一度音声を聞いて，答えの根拠となる使役文の（　　）を埋めなさい。

1. The turbulence (　　　　　　　　　).
2. And now, ladies and gentleman, for my final trick, I'll (　　　　　　　　)
disappear.
3. Because this medicine might (　　　　　　　　).

TASK

Key Sentences for Writing を使って，図書館で小さい子供への注意書きを作りましょう（99 ページ）。小さい子供たちは字が読めません。次の文を参考に，保護者に対する注意書きにする必要があります。
● Don't run in the library. → Don't let your child run in the library.

UNIT 16 — My History

自分史を書く

完了形

Key Sentences for Writing 62

- I have never been to China.
- I have been learning English since I was 12 years old.

Warm-Up 63

下の文章は Aunt Mary の自分史です。完了形が使われている部分に下線を引きなさい。

I was born and raised in China. When I was 12 years old, our family emigrated to San Francisco in the United States. I have been here for 60 years. When I was 24, I fell in love with Pat and married him. We had a happy life. Unfortunately he passed away seven years ago, and I have lived in this house alone since then. But I have never felt lonely. Three children and nine grandchildren live in my neighborhood. Moreover I have a lot of close friends here and we have been learning some languages and the piano together. I really enjoy it. My only dream is to visit my hometown in China again. I have never been back to China since I left.

注) emigrate 移民する

Grammar for Writing 64

現在完了形

現在完了とは，過去のことでも現在のことでもなく，過去から現在へ至る出来事を表すために使う時制です。形は「**have ＋ 動詞の過去分詞**」です。現在形や過去形が今や昔のある一時点のことだけを表すのに対して，現在完了形は過去から現在までの時間の幅をもった出来事や状態を表します。現在完了形には大きく次の３つの用法があります。

（1）継続「ずっと…している」
過去のある時点から始まった動作や状態が今まで続いていることを表します。
- I **have been** here for 60 years.
- I **have not** seen him recently.

（2）経験「…したことがある」
現在に至るまでの経験を表します。
- I **have visited** China three times.
- My sister **has** never **been** absent from school.

(3) 完了「(たった今) …したところだ」

ある動作や状態が完了して今に至っていることを表します。

- I **have** just **finished** an advanced class.
- He **has** not **arrived** yet.

📋 現在完了進行形

「**have been + -ing 形の動詞**」で，「ずっと…し続けている」という意味を表します。

- I **have been learning** Japanese since I was 10.
- Tom **has been playing** computer games for three hours.

📋 過去完了

過去のある時点を基準にして，それ以前からそれまでの時間の流れの中での出来事を表す時制です。現在完了と同じように，継続，経験，完了の意味があります。

- He **had been** busy till yesterday. (継続)
  (「昨日」の時点まで忙しい状態が続いていたことを表しています)

- I realized that I **had seen** him before. (経験)
  (「気づいた」時点 (過去) までの経験を表しています)

- I **had** just **finished** my dinner when the telephone rang. (完了)
  (「電話が鳴った」時点ですでに食事が終わっていたことを表しています)

✅ VOCABULARY FOR WRITING

◆現在完了形の文には，時に関する表現がよく使われます。

- for… (…の間)　　　　　　I have known Jack **for more than 10 years**.
- since… (…以来)　　　　　I have had a stomachache **since yesterday**.
- before (以前)　　　　　　I have watched this movie **before**.
- ever (今まで)　　　　　　Have you **ever** been to Canada?
- yet (もう，まだ)　　　　　Have you finished the assignment **yet**?—No, not **yet**.
- already (すでに)　　　　　I have **already** finished my assignment.
- just (ちょうど，たった今)　I have **just** received your mail.

1 （　　）の中の指示に従って文を書き換えなさい。

1. I finished my homework. （just を加えて「ちょうど終えた」という意味に）

2. I am busy. （since yesterday を加えて「昨日からずっと忙しい」という意味に）

3. I did not go to Hawaii. （before を加えて「行ったことがない」という意味に）

4. Did you see a movie star in Hollywood? （ever を加えて「見たことある？」という意味に）

5. He spent more than 1 million yen on his car. （at that time を入れて過去完了で，「百万円も使っていた」という意味に）

6. They did not finish their job. （when I left the office を加えて過去完了で，「終えていなかった」という意味に）

7. The children are watching TV. （for two hours を加えて現在完了進行形で，「ずっとテレビを見ている」という意味に）

2 （　　）内の語句を使って，次の日本語の意味を表す英文を書きなさい。ただし，動詞は適当な形に変える必要があります。

1. 彼女は 3 日間何も食べていない。 （anything, for three days）

2. あなたはどれくらいの間ここにいるのですか。 （how long, be here）

3. 今まで沖縄に行ったことはありますか。 （ever）

4. 1 週間ずっと雨が続いている。 （it, rain, for a week）

5. 私たちはあなたのことをあちこち探していたのよ。 （everywhere, look for）

6. 帰ってきたら，母はすでに買い物に出かけてしまっていた。 （when I came home, go shopping）

3 次の各文の誤りを直しなさい。

1. Have you lived in Osaka 10 years ago?

2. I have been looking for this book from last year.

3. I have never gone to Australia before.

4. Kim has studied English for two years before she came to England.

5. Tom has seen the man when he was a boy.

音声を聞いて正解を確認しましょう。 65

4 Cameron の生い立ちを聞いて，下の年表を完成させなさい。 66

YEAR	
1970	Born in (　　　　　　　)
(　　　)	Moved to California
1976–1982	Elementary school
	■ played (　　　　) for six years
	■ visited Grandmother in Japan (　　) times
1983–1989	High school
	■ met (　　　　　)
(　　　)	Got married
2004	Earned a (　　　) degree

TASK

問題4を参考に，99ページの左の年表にあなたのこれまでの経歴を書きなさい。それを参考に右に自分史を書いてみましょう。できるだけ現在完了形を使ってみましょう。

Introducing Japanese Culture

日本文化を
紹介する

関係代名詞

- Mary is an American girl who loves Japanese art.
- This is the first novel that was written by Natsume Soseki.

 68

以下は日本を紹介するガイドブックの中のコラムです。A，B はどんな食べ物でしょうか。また関係代名詞が使われている箇所に下線を引きなさい。

Traditional Food in Japan

Do you know (**A**)? Japanese people often recommend us foreigners to try (**A**).

(**A**) is a traditional Japanese food made from fermented soy beans. It smells like rotten beans. If you smell it, you will never think it is a food. But actually it is a very healthy and popular food that Japanese often eat for breakfast. In addition to (**A**), do not forget to try (**B**). It is pickled squid which is prepared with its organs and salt. It goes perfectly with sake. Sake is a popular alcoholic drink made from rice. Enjoy some traditional Japanese food!

注）fermented 発酵した　rotten 腐った　squid イカ　organs 内臓

A: _____　　B: _____

Grammar for Writing 69

関係代名詞

関係代名詞とは，名前のとおり，2 つの文を関係付けて結び付ける接続詞の役割をもった代名詞のことです。

- *Natto* is a traditional Japanese food. + **And** **it** is made from fermented soy beans.
- *Natto* is a traditional Japanese food **which** is made from fermented soy beans.

　　　　　先行詞　　　　　関係代名詞

関係代名詞に続く節（which is made from fermented soy beans）が，それに先行する語句（a traditional Japanese food）を修飾する関係になります。関係代名詞が修飾する名詞を先行詞と呼びます。先行詞が人の場合とものの場合で異なる関係代名詞が使われます。

先行詞が人の場合
関係代名詞 **who, whose, whom** を使用します。

- Mary is <u>an American girl</u> **who** loves Japanese art.（主格）

- That is <u>the boy</u> **whose** father is famous as a movie director.（所有格）

- <u>The politician</u> (**whom**) we met a week ago was killed by a terrorist.（目的格）

  ＊ whom は省略されるか，who で代用されることがほとんどです。

先行詞がものの場合
代名詞の格にかかわらず **which** を使用します。

- *Shiokara* is <u>pickled squid</u> **which** is prepared with its organs and salt.
  （主格）

- *Kadomatsu* is <u>an ornament</u> **which** we use to celebrate a new year.
  （目的格）

なお関係代名詞 **that** は先行詞が人であっても，ものであっても使用することができます。

- *Merutomo* is <u>a new word</u> **that** young people use to refer to a friend they

  communicate with via the Internet.

Tips for Writing

先行詞に最上級，the only，the first，the same などが使用される場合は，関係代名詞 that が好んで使われます。
- This is the first novel **that** was written by Haruki Murakami.
- He is the most experienced doctor **that** I have met in my life.

EXERCISE

1 ( ) 内に適当な関係代名詞を入れなさい。

1. Disneyland is a famous amusement park ( ) was built by Walt Disney.

2. The politician ( ) was arrested yesterday was from Hokkaido.

3. The children ( ) parents smoke are at a risk of cancer.

4. I saw the famous Hollywood star ( ) I wanted to see for a long time.

5. This is the garden ( ) my grandmother made when she was alive.

6. Ken is the only student ( ) can speak English fluently in this class.

2 関係代名詞を使って 2 つの文をひとつにしなさい。

1. I have an uncle. He lives in Paris.

2. This is the famous picture. It won the first prize at the contest.

3. Mr. Tsuji is a wonderful novelist. His books are very popular among young people.

4. The movie was not interesting at all. I saw it yesterday.

5. Tom was the only boy. I could trust him.

3 ( ) 内の単語を並べ換えて文を完成させなさい。

1. *Hinamatsuri* is (for girls / is / a / festival / which / held) in March.

2. Kamakura is an old capital (many Japanese people / is / loved / which / by).

3. *Gokon* is a kind of party (find / have / a boyfriend [girlfriend] / that / young people / in order to).

4 ( ) 内の語句を参考にして，関係代名詞を使って，次の文の続きを説明しなさい。

1. What is *sumo*? (hint: popular)
It is a sport _____.

2. Do you know what a *yukata* is? (hint: wear / summer)
It is a kind of kimono _____.

3. Could you tell me what *katsuobushi* is? (hint: dried fish / soup stock)

It is _____ .

5 音声を聞いて，各文が説明しているものを下から選びなさい。 70

1. _____   2. _____   3. _____   4. _____   5. _____

a.

b.

c.

d.

e.

f.

g.

h.

T A S K

下の中から好きなテーマを選び，Key Sentences for Writing を参考に，関係代名詞を使って，
101 ページのタスクシートにその説明を書いてみましょう。

a

b

c

d

If I were . . .

仮定の(＝現実でない)話を
書く

仮定法

Key Sentences for Writing

- If I won 10 million yen in the lottery, I would donate it to the Red Cross.
- I wish I had more free time.

 **Warm-Up** 🔊 72

心理テストです。次の質問に答えてください。

Q1. If you called your boyfriend/girlfriend and he/she did not answer, what would you do?

  A. I would call him/her again and again until he/she answered.

  B. I would think he/she was sleeping.

  C. I would leave a message asking him/her to call back.

Q2. If you scored 50 on an English test, what would you do?

  A. I would review my errors so that I would not repeat the same mistakes.

  B. I would decide to study harder from next week.

  C. I would feel down about my grades.

Q3. If you had only 1,000 yen for the following three day's food, what would you do?

  A. I would feel down about my budget and lose my appetite.

  B. I would spend 300 yen on each day's food.

  C. I wouldn't care about how much I had and eat anything I wanted to eat.

あなたの回答のポイントを下の表から求め，その合計を出してみましょう。結果は 71 ページを見てください。

	Q1	Q2	Q3
A	1	2	1
B	3	3	2
C	2	1	3

例) Q1-A, Q2-B, Q3-C
  1 + 3 + 3 = 7（合計ポイント）

 Grammar for Writing 🔊 73

📋 **仮定法**

英語の仮定法を正しく使うポイントは，前後の節の動詞の形をそろえることです。

仮定法過去：事実に反する現在の仮定を表します。

- If I **were** rich, I **would/could** buy the car.（実際には金持ちではない）

● If I **had** more money, I **could** buy the car.（実際には持っていない）

前の節が過去形（be 動詞は were になることに注意）
⇨ 後ろの節も過去形（will や can の過去形である would/could）

「現在のこと」を言う場合には「過去形」を使う，というのに少し違和感を持つかもしれませんが，日本語でも同じように「過去形」を使っています。たとえば，「もしひまだったら行けるんだけど，残念だなあ」はどうでしょうか。「ひまだったら」と過去形にしていますね。

仮定法過去完了：事実に反する過去の仮定を表します。
● If I **had studied** more, I **would have** passed the exam.
（実際は勉強しなかった）
● If you **had listened** to my advice, you **wouldn't have** had so many problems.
（実際には聞かなかった）
前の節が過去完了（**had** + 過去分詞）⇨ 後ろの節も **would have** + 過去分詞

仮定法現在：未来の仮定を表します。
● If it **is** fine tomorrow, I **will** take a walk in the morning.
● If we **miss** the last train, we **will** have to walk home.
前の節が現在形 ⇨ 後ろの節は未来形

仮定の対象となることがらの時間と，if 節の動詞の形の関係を整理すると次のようになります。

過去のこと	現在のこと	未来のこと
↓	↓	↓
過去完了形	過去形	現在形

Tips for Writing

「…だといいなあ」 希望や期待を表す場合は，主語が自分自身の希望は hope + to 不定詞，自分以外の場合は hope + that . . . で表します。
● I **hope to** study abroad.
● I **hope** you will like my presents.
「…だったらいいのに」 非現実的な，不可能に近い願望を表す場合は，wish を使います。be 動詞の場合は were になることに注意しましょう。
● I **wish** Kimutaku **were** here.
● I **wish** I **were** richer.
● I **wish** my boyfriend **had** a car.

《心理テストの結果分析》
total points
7–9　　You are optimistic and easygoing. How happy you are!
4–6　　You are realistic and rationalistic.
3　　You are pessimistic. Take it easy!

1 次の各文の下線部を適当な形に変えなさい。そして，それぞれの文を日本語に訳しなさい。

1. I wish there <u>be</u> more time. (　　　　　)
日本語訳：＿＿＿＿＿＿＿＿＿＿＿＿＿＿＿＿＿＿＿＿＿＿＿＿

2. I wouldn't say if it <u>be</u> not true. (　　　　　)
日本語訳：＿＿＿＿＿＿＿＿＿＿＿＿＿＿＿＿＿＿＿＿＿＿＿＿

3. I would not sign the contract even if I <u>be</u> you. (　　　　　)
日本語訳：＿＿＿＿＿＿＿＿＿＿＿＿＿＿＿＿＿＿＿＿＿＿＿＿

4. I wish I <u>have</u> more time. (　　　　　)
日本語訳：＿＿＿＿＿＿＿＿＿＿＿＿＿＿＿＿＿＿＿＿＿＿＿＿

5. If I <u>have</u> my credit card in my wallet yesterday, I <u>can buy</u> the dress.
(　　　　　) (　　　　　)
日本語訳：＿＿＿＿＿＿＿＿＿＿＿＿＿＿＿＿＿＿＿＿＿＿＿＿

6. If it <u>be</u> sunny this weekend, I <u>go</u> hiking. (　　　　　) (　　　　　)
日本語訳：＿＿＿＿＿＿＿＿＿＿＿＿＿＿＿＿＿＿＿＿＿＿＿＿

7. If I <u>take</u> medicine yesterday, I <u>will be</u> better now. (　　　　　) (　　　　　)
日本語訳：＿＿＿＿＿＿＿＿＿＿＿＿＿＿＿＿＿＿＿＿＿＿＿＿

8. If I <u>know</u> his e-mail address, I <u>can give</u> it to you. (　　　　　)
(　　　　　)
日本語訳：＿＿＿＿＿＿＿＿＿＿＿＿＿＿＿＿＿＿＿＿＿＿＿＿

9. If it <u>not snow</u> yesterday, I <u>can wash</u> my car. (　　　　　) (　　　　　)
日本語訳：＿＿＿＿＿＿＿＿＿＿＿＿＿＿＿＿＿＿＿＿＿＿＿＿

10. If I <u>be not tired</u>, I <u>go</u> to the party last night. (　　　　　) (　　　　　)
日本語訳：＿＿＿＿＿＿＿＿＿＿＿＿＿＿＿＿＿＿＿＿＿＿＿＿

2 (　　) 内の語句を並べ替えて文を完成させなさい。そして，それぞれの文を日本語に訳しなさい。

1. If (woken / earlier / had / I / a little / up), (missed / not / bus / would / I / have / the usual).
日本語訳：＿＿＿＿＿＿＿＿＿＿＿＿＿＿＿＿＿＿＿＿＿＿＿＿

2. I (during / done / wish / had / I / the winter / exercise / more / a little).
日本語訳：＿＿＿＿＿＿＿＿＿＿＿＿＿＿＿＿＿＿＿＿＿＿＿＿

3. I wish (fluently / I / speak / could / French).
日本語訳：＿＿＿＿＿＿＿＿＿＿＿＿＿＿＿＿＿＿＿＿＿＿＿＿

4. If (more / time / free / had / I), (her / I / a date / could / for / ask).

日本語訳：_____

5. If (studied / had / I / harder), (the exam / I / passed / have / could).

日本語訳：_____

6. If (not / it / rained / had), (gone / we / hiking / have / could / together).

日本語訳：_____

✓ 3 （　　）内の語句を使って，日本語の意味を表す英文を書きなさい。

1. 英語がうまく話せればなあ。(fluently)

2. もっと一生懸命勉強していれば単位を取れていたのに。(I / take the credit)

3. もし雨が降っていなければ，バーベキューができたのに。(have a barbecue party)

4. もう少し早く起きていればいつもの電車に乗れたのに。(I / catch the usual train)

5. 車を持っていれば彼女をデートに誘えるのに。(I)

6. 夏の間にもう少し体を鍛えておけばよかった。(I)

⬚ TASK

もし宝くじで 1000 万円当たったらどうしますか。Key Sentences for Writing を応用して 101 ページのタスクシートに仮定法を用いて文を 5 つ書いてみましょう。
If I won 10 million yen in the lottery, I would…

UNIT 19 Expressing Your Opinion 考えを伝える

節・間接疑問文

> **Key Sentences for Writing**
> - I remember that Japan was hit by an earthquake in 2011.
> - I cannot say if the information is correct or not.

Warm-Up 75

次のコラムを読み，節の部分に下線を引いてみましょう。

Do you remember that Japan was hit by a huge earthquake in 2011? In Fukushima, nuclear power plants were terribly damaged by tsunamis. Since then, people have started to doubt if nuclear power is cheap and safe. Some people say that we should introduce safer energy like solar and wind power. Other people, however, believe nuclear power is necessary for the development of our industry. It is very difficult to say which is correct. What do you think of this issue?

Grammar for Writing 76

📄 節

節とは主語と動詞を含んだひとかたまりの語群を言います。that や疑問詞に導かれた節は，名詞のように文の目的語や補語，あるいは主語として機能します。

that に続く節：「…ということ」
- It is a good idea. + I think so.
  I think **that** it is a good idea . （that 以下が think の目的語）
- I did not know **that** she was married . （that 以下が know の目的語）

接続詞 that は省略されることがよくあります。
- I don't think he is telling a lie .
- I believe he will do his best .

whether/if に続く節：「…かどうか」
- Does Tom still love her? + I don't know that.
  I don't know **whether** Tom still loves her .

- She asked whether I liked classical music . （目的語）
- The question is whether Tom still loves her . （補語）
- Whether the system will work or not entirely depends on him. （主語）

接続詞 whether の代わりに if を使うことも可能です。また，文末に or not を付けることもあります。

- I cannot say if (whether) the information is correct or not .
- He was not sure if (whether) he could keep the secret or not .

疑問詞に続く節：when, where, what, who, how, which など

- When was Todaiji built? + Everybody knows that.
  Everybody knows when Todaiji was built . （when 以下が know の目的語）

疑問文が節になる場合を**間接疑問文**と呼ぶことがあります。その場合は，語順に注意する必要があります。疑問文では be 動詞や助動詞が主語の前に来ますね（When **was To-daiji** built?）。しかし，節になるともはや疑問文ではなくなるため，肯定文と同じ語順になります（Everybody knows when **Todaiji was** built.）。

- I wonder where I can find the book .
- Bob did not know what he should say to her .

✅ VOCABULARY FOR WRITING

◆節を使って自分の意見を述べる

英語で自分の意見を述べる際，日本人は I think . . . をよく使いますが，それ以外の表現も覚えておくと便利です。

- I believe that / I am sure that . . . （確信）
  I don't believe she is telling the truth.
- I hope that . . . （希望）
  I just hope that their meeting is going well.
- I am afraid that . . . （懸念）
  I'm afraid that I can't accept your offer.
- I agree that . . . （賛成・同意）
  I agree that we should celebrate this event.
- It seems to me that . . . （推測）
  It seems to me that this is the most important issue.

✓1 節の部分に下線を引きなさい。

1. I think that Mr. Tanaka is the best person to be the next president.

2. I don't know if I should accept the offer or not.

3. I am not even sure whether Tom is still alive or not.

4. I really want to know who won the game.

5. Whether I am fired or not is a very big problem for my family.

✓2 (　　) の中に適切な語を下から選んで入れなさい。何も入れる必要のないときは×を入れなさい。

1. I just cannot believe (　　　　) they could finish the work so soon.

2. I wonder (　　　) it was wise to let her travel alone.

3. We were shocked to learn (　　　) Professor Smith had got cancer.

4. He did not remember (　　　) he left his wallet.

5. (　　　) his story is true or false does not matter to me.

6. I cannot agree (　　　) we have to pay so much consumption tax.

7. I am not sure (　　　) which is the better plan for our project.

that　whether　if　what　where　when

✓3 2つの文を，節を使ってひとつにしなさい。

1. Japanese elementary schools introduced a five-day week. I agree with that.

2. When is his birthday? I don't know that.

3. How can I get to the department store? Do you know?

4. Can you speak Spanish? I asked Tom.

5. The temperature of the earth is getting warmer and warmer. It is true.

✓ 4 下の文を読み，日本語の意味になるように反論を書きなさい。

1. A: I like the cafeteria in this university. I think it's great. What do you think?

B: おいしい（the food is good）とは思うけどちょっと高い（a little expensive）と思うな。

I agree that _____ .

2. A: I think that women should stay home and do housework.

B: 悪いけど（I'm afraid）あなたの考えは時代遅れ（out of fashion）だと思う。

_____ .

3. A: I think the Japanese Prime Minister is doing very well. Don't you agree?

B: 彼が適任（the best person）とは思えないね。

_____ .

5 次の会話を聞いて，（　　）を聞き取って記入しましょう。 🔊 77

1. A: Tom is still working on the report. What do you think?

B: I don't think (　　　　　　　　　　　　) on time.

2. A: It's freezing outside. Where did those clouds come from?

B: I know. I'm (　　　　　　　　　　) this afternoon.

3. A: They are saying that we will need another nuclear power plant.

B: That's ridiculous. I (　　　　　　　　　　),
but it doesn't have to be nuclear-powered.

4. A: She's playing in the final of the championship tonight.

B: (　　　　　　　　　　).

TASK

現在，日本の小学校では英語を教えています。下の文を読んで 103 ページにあなたの賛成，または反対意見を書きましょう。また，その理由も書いてみましょう。Vocabulary for Writing を参考にするとよいでしょう。

In Japanese primary schools, pupils learn English conversation. They have English classes a few times a month. What do you think about this new curriculum?

78

Key Sentences for Writing

- Although it is only a 10-minute walk, it is a little complicated.
- First write your name. Then answer the questions.

Warm-Up 79

これは Mami と日本に来たばかりの Kate とのメールのやり取りです。Kate の家から歌舞伎座までの道順を下に記入しなさい。

Hi Kate,

To get to Kabuki-za, you should first walk to Shimo-kitazawa Station and take the Odakyu Line to Shinjuku. Next, change trains at Shinjuku. Then go to Shimbashi or Yuraku-cho on the JR Line. You can walk to Kabuki-za from both stations. Although it is only a 10-minute walk, it is a little complicated. Kabuki-za is on the corner of Harumi Street and Showa Street. Have a good day!

Mami

Hi Mami,

I am going to watch Kabuki tomorrow. Could you please tell me the way to the Kabuki-za theater from my apartment?

Kate

家 → (　　　　　) → (　　　　　)

→ (　　　or　　　) → 歌舞伎座

Grammar for Writing 80

📋 接続詞

接続詞とは単語と単語，句と句，節と節をつなぎ合わせる語句を言います。

- I saw ｜Mary｜ **and** ｜Tom｜ talking on the street. （単語と単語）
- Usually I spend my weekend ｜watching videos｜ **or** ｜playing tennis｜. （句と句）
- **When** ｜you feel dizzy｜, ｜don't take a bath｜. （節と節）

接続詞には，上記のもの以外にもさまざまなものがあります。そのいくつかの例を見てみましょう。

逆接を表す but / yet

- She's 80 years old, **but** she goes swimming every day.
- The weather was cold, **yet** bright and sunny.

理由を表す because / since / as / for

- We went by bus **because** it was cheaper.

- **Since** there was no more work to do, we all went home.
- **As** it was getting late, we took the children home.
- I decided to go to sleep, **for** I was very tired.

時を表す as soon as / before / after / while / since
- **As soon as** we arrived at the hotel, it started raining.
- Think carefully **before** you decide.
- **After** you had left, I had a phone call from Peter.
- Could you take care of the children **while** I prepare lunch?
- He had been composing music **since** he was 12 years old.

譲歩を表す although / (even) though
- **Although (Though)** she was tired, she could not sleep.

条件を表す if / in case / unless
- **In case (If)** you can't come, give me a call before noon.
- The car should be in the garage **unless** someone has moved it.

transitional adverb

文と文との流れをわかりやすくつないでくれる副詞（句）を **transitional adverb** と言います。

順序を表す副詞：first / second / last / next / then など
- **First** write your name. **Then** answer the questions.

逆接や対照を表す副詞：however / on the other hand など
- The teacher gave the students some hints. Some of them, **however**, could not answer the question.
- Tom is very curious and wants to know everything about others. **On the other hand**, his brother is not interested in others.

接続詞も transitional adverb も，語，句，節，文などのつながりや話の流れをわかりやすくする機能をもっています。

 VOCABULARY FOR WRITING

◆道案内の表現

道順を表す表現には次のようなものがあります。
- Go straight. ● Turn left at the next corner. ● Go two blocks and turn right.
- Make a right turn at the bank. ● Cross the bridge. ● Cross the street.
- It is next to the bank. ● It is across from the bank. ● It is on your right.
- It is at the end of the street. ● It is on the corner of 5th Street and Lincoln Avenue.

✓1 (　　) 中に適切な接続詞を書き入れなさい。

1. Do you know the girl over there wearing glasses (　　　　　) a hat?

2. Which would you like to have, beef steak (　　　　　) roast chicken?

3. Mary is an intelligent girl, (　　　　　) she's very lazy.

4. The game was canceled (　　　　　) it started to snow.

5. (　　　　　) he has got a good job now, he still complains.

6. I was taking a shower (　　　　　) she called.

7. I can bring it to you (　　　　　) you want.

8. Clean up this mess (　　　　　) your father sees it.

✓2 接続詞を使ってひとつの文にしなさい。

1. He did not agree to the plan. It was approved by the committee.

2. Mary often tells a lie. No one believes what she says.

3. Tom was doing his work. His dog was sleeping quietly beside him.

4. Be sure to get up early. You don't want to be late for the exam.

5. He does not stop smoking. He will suffer from lung cancer. （unless を使って）

✓3 下の地図を見て英語で道案内をしなさい。

1. (　　　　　　　　　　　　), and (　　　　　　　　　　　　　).

2. (　　　　　　　　　　　). Then it's (　　　　　　　　　　　　　).

3. First, (　　　　　　　　　　　　　　) at the school, then

　(　　　　　　　　　　　　　　) blocks.

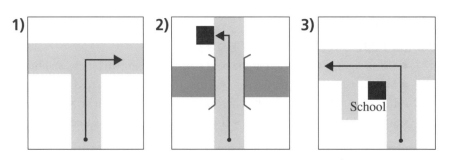

4 以下はホノルルの地図です。あなたはハレクラニホテル（Halekulani Hotel）に泊まっています。そこから，音声の指示に従って出かけるとどこに着くか聞き取りなさい。

81

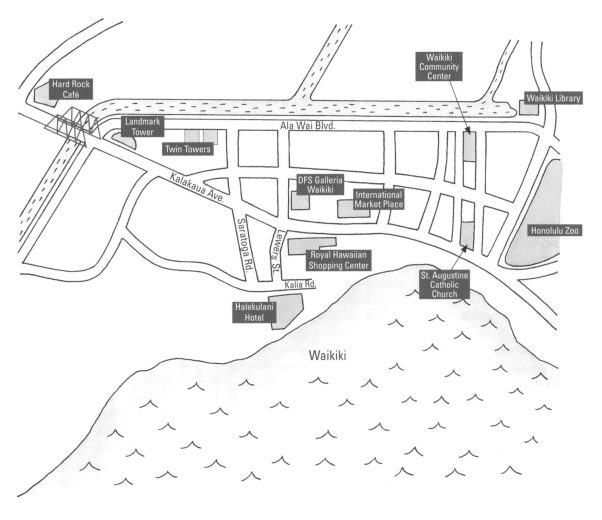

TASK

上記のホノルルの地図を見て，ハレクラニホテルから以下の場所への行き方を，接続詞や transitional adverb を使って説明しなさい（103 ページ）。Vocabulary for Writing を参考にしましょう。

1. Hard Rock Café
2. DFS Galleria Waikiki
3. Waikiki Library

タスクシート

Number	Name	Date
		/ /

キリトリ線

Number	Name	Date
		/ /

My Dream Room

I'll explain about my dream room.

_____

_____

_____

_____

_____

_____

_____

Your Partner's Dream Room

Number	Name	Date
		/ /

----------------- キリトリ線 -----------------

Schedule for _____ (date)

AM

PM

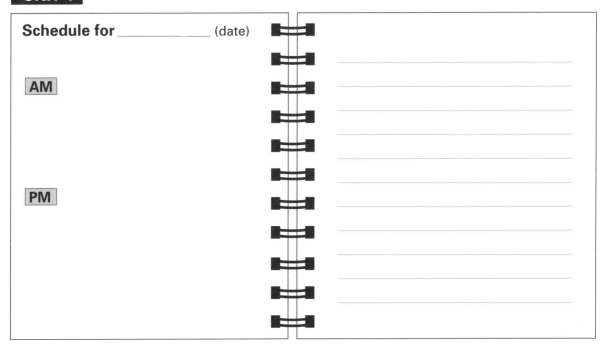

Number	Name	Date
		/ /

Miso Soup

For   servings

Preparation Time: mins.

Ingredients:

How to cook:

Number	Name	Date
		/ /

キリトリ線

UNIT 6

Number	Name	Date
		/ /

UNIT 7

Number	Name		Date
			/ /

- キリトリ線 -

UNIT 8

Diary Date: _____

Number	Name	Date
		/ /

UNIT 9

Number	Name	Date
		/ /

------------------------------------ キリトリ線 ------------------------------------

UNIT 10

Number	Name	Date
		/ /

UNIT 11

Name: _____
          (family name)

_____
          (given name)

Birthday: _____

Age: _____   **Sex:** ☐ M ☐ F

Phone Number: _____
                          (home)

_____
             (mobile)

E-mail Address: _____

Skills:

Number	Name	Date
		/ /

- - - キリトリ線 - - -

UNIT 12

Number	Name	Date
		/ /

UNIT 13

Subject :

CC :

Number	Name	Date
		/ /

- - - - - - - - キリトリ線 - - - - - - - -

UNIT 14

Number	Name	Date
		/ /

UNIT 15

NOTICE

Number	Name	Date
		/ /

- - - - - - - - - - - - - - - - - - キリトリ線 - - - - - - - - - - - - - - - - - - -

UNIT 16

Age	Event		My History

Number	Name	Date
		/ /

UNIT 17

Theme: _____

Number	Name	Date
		/ /

- - - - - - - - - - - - - - - - - - キリトリ線 - - - - - - - - - - - - - - - -

UNIT 18

1

2

3

4

5

Number	Name	Date
		/ /

UNIT 19

Number	Name	Date
		/ /

- キリトリ線 -

UNIT 20

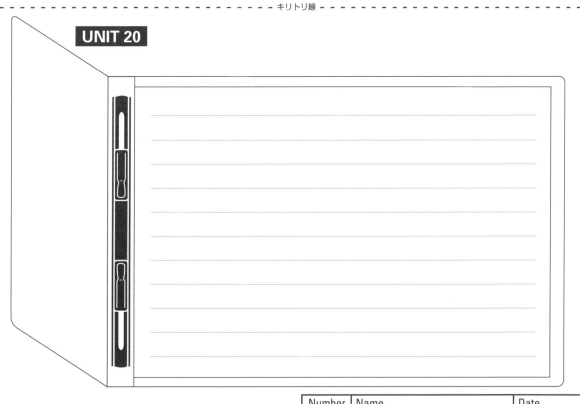

Number	Name	Date
		/ /

本書には音声 CD（別売）があります

New English Composition Workbook
—For Functional Writing Skills

新・発信型英作文

2021 年 1 月 20 日　初版第 1 刷発行
2023 年 2 月 20 日　初版第 4 刷発行

　著　者　　村 田 和 代
　　　　　　大 谷 麻 美

　発行者　　福 岡 正 人
　発行所　　株式会社　**金 星 堂**
（〒 101-0051）東京都千代田区神田神保町 3-21
Tel. (03) 3263-3828（営業部）
　 (03) 3263-3997（編集部）
Fax (03) 3263-0716
http://www.kinsei-do.co.jp

編集担当　長島吉成　　　　　　　　　　Printed in Japan
印刷所・製本所／株式会社カショ
ISBN978-4-7647-4128-7　　C1082